Laura Enjoy!!

Mom from Ireland 2015

A Pinch of This...

Tastes of
Home Cooking
with

Frank Moynihan

D1502512

on STREAM

Published by On Stream Publications Ltd
Cloghroe, Blarney, County Cork, Ireland
Tel/fax + 353 21 438 5798
email: info@onstream.ie
web: www.onstream.ie

Recipes © Frank Moynihan

Food Photographs: Norma Cuddihy
Back cover photograph: Don McMonagle
Book Design: Nick at On Stream
Editor: Roz Crowley

ISBN: 978 1 897685 82 2

A CIP catalogue record of this book is available from the British Library.

The moral right of the author has been asserted.

CONTENTS

INTRODUCTION

"Write a cookery book!" I was told again and again. Yes, but for whom? The world is not short of glossy, overpriced editions with little other than nice photographs of dishes which never turn out the way they look when cooked at home. It is my experience that 80% of cookery books are never opened after the first browse through.

Yes, I would love to go to print, but not to be yet another subscriber to the above mentioned volumes. So, my cookery book will be simple to follow, with everyday ingredients for everyday people and above all, it will be about economy.

How many domestic caterers sit down at home for 15 minutes one evening a week to plan out the coming week's family menu? And how many stock-take their larders to see what is required, making out a shopping list based on those requirements only? This is the first elementary step to economising and providing your family with better and more varied food.

When attempting to do this the first time, make out a list of the main course dishes and vegetables, remembering to vary the methods of cooking as much as possible — roasting, stewing, frying, grilling. Keep the liquid left over from a boiled chicken to form the base for many starters, soups or sauces later on in the week. Do not throw away the carcass, raw or cooked, as it will make excellent stock.

You must never have food left over. I operated a small restaurant on the island of Inis Meáin in the Aran Islands from June to September every year for six years. During the high season, we did about 20 dinners each evening and we did not have a rubbish bin. This was managed by taking the customer's order for the evening meal at the time of booking (I have never met a customer who was not happy to do this), then, to cook only the exact requirements for the amount of persons booked. We served simple food cooked with loving tender care, and we never had a complaint in six years.

Vegetables or potato dishes were cooked to order

(vegetables were usually stir-fried or lightly steamed) as were all main courses. The only advance cooking done at An Dún restaurant were soups and casseroles whose flavours were enhanced with time.

Welcome to the pages of "A Pinch of This..." Follow the advice herein, and you can take my word you will save yourself a minimum of €50 per week on food costs, as well as the joy of knowing that your family is benefiting from your new approach to everyday cooking.

"Not in the costly savour lies the greatest pleasure." So wrote Horace, and I entirely agree with his sentiments which were echoed in two unique experiences of two people from two very different backgrounds as they sat down to the day's main meal, in two entirely different atmospheres:

I was visiting the home of Peadar O'Conghaile on Inis Meáin, one beautiful June day in 1994, when he had just returned from the field where he had spent six hours "spraying the garden." Peadar's wife, Maura, set out on the table before him two boiled, salted mackerel with lovely green cabbage from the garden at the side of the house, and eight large island-produced potatoes, boiled in their jackets. Having fervently bowed his head and given thanks to God, Peadar devoured all before him with only the occasional moan of satisfaction. This was washed down with a large mug of milk after which he wiped the sleeve of his jumper across his lips and replaced his cap on his head. After the sign of the cross followed the shortest of prayers in Irish, Moladh go deo le Dia, he busily filled his pipe to answer its imperial behests.

That very evening, I was visited in my restaurant by a very important lady. This person, who shall remain nameless, sat down to a meal of crab cakes with a mussel and carrageen sauce, followed by a seafood broth. The main course included a mousse of prawn and periwinkle wrapped in wild smoked salmon. This meal was consumed with rather slower and measured forkfuls, and even though enjoyed to the limit, no one component was entirely finished. Looking back that night over my two experiences, I felt Peadar was the one with the greatest meal enjoyment, and Maura was the one with the most Customer Satisfaction. "Not in the costly savour lies the greatest pleasure," and Peadar's cost-free mackerel gave the greatest pleasure of the two meals.

Do not take out your food fetishes on your children. Instead, introduce them to varied foods, correctly cooked — they will be eternally grateful to you and you will see the budget stretch.

Professional cooks know the importance of menu planning and this is an important step at domestic level too; you know the number of people you have to feed, how many meals per day, and their likes and dislikes. You also know the amount of cash available to you to put food on your table for the coming week so good planning is possible.

Start by talking to the members of your family, tell them what you are proposing to do and seek their assistance - you will be amazed, it will be forthcoming. You must also tell them that in the interest of balance and nutrition, foods that heretofore they did not particularly like, may be reappearing on your new menu cycle. Point out to them the importance of giving such foods at least one more try. Also explain to your offspring the common sense of eating three meals per day, no junk food in between. You will not arrive at instant success on this one, but even a small reduction in the amount of junk is to be welcomed and encouraged; providing them with good alternatives will keep hunger at bay.

Next, sit down and make lists of meals, dishes and ingredients, allowing yourself €75 to feed the family for the next 7 days. Restrict meat on your menus to not more than 4 days. Introduce the cheapest fish you can buy, at least 3 times a week, and have a vegetarian dish one day a week.

Never buy frozen chips, they are too expensive. Restrict the use of chips (your home-made) to one day per week using unpeeled potatoes. A new alternative is to use wedges of unpeeled potatoes sprinkled with Schwartz potato wedge coating to spice them up and bake them in the oven. A simple but effective idea.

Whatever you do in life - by trade, profession, vocation, or just living and travelling the road of fortune, one thing is for sure: you must get the basics right.

This of course is especially true of cooking. Identify and understand the basic methods of cooking (i.e. boiling, poaching, steaming, roasting, baking, stewing, grilling, frying and braising) then get the basic methods of making stock and sauces and you are well on your way to having your own TV show or writing your own cook book.

I teach cookery classes from October to May every year and on the first night I always pose the question: "If one was to poach a chicken for lunch, should the chicken be put into cold, warm, hot or boiling water?" And what about roasted meats? How many roasts are put into cold ovens every Sunday resulting in juice loss and ultimately, loss of flavour and volume of meat?

The home cook who goes to the little trouble of making a home-produced stock will be rewarded with beautiful soups, sauces, gravies and stews, dishes with individual flavour and a heavier purse on the way home from the weekly trip to the supermarket.

Then, there's the all-important matter of portion size, how much do I cook for my family? Getting this right will really save money and is there anything more rewarding to the cook than empty plates, empty saucepans and an empty rubbish bin? The ultimate signs of success!

START THE DAY RIGHT - EAT A BREAKFAST

Without any doubt, breakfast is the most important meal of the day. When I was young, my mother was out of bed each and every morning at 7.30 to prepare breakfast for her working husband and 9 school-going children.

A bowl of steaming porridge for everybody each morning plus a boiled egg when the household budget allowed, was complemented with home-made brown bread and a mug of steaming tea.

Today's supermarket shelves are laden down with all sorts of breakfast cereal and all undoubtedly have merit, but in my opinion, none will ever take the place of a bowl of porridge.

For perfect porridge, soak 2 cups of porridge oatlets overnight in 4 cups of cold water with 1 cup of milk and a little salt. Bring to the boil next morning and simmer for 2 minutes. Serve immediately, small portions at first, and watch them lap it up. Children who partake of this each morning with a hot beverage plus a slice of buttered toast or brown bread are set up for the day and will not be distracted by hunger pangs 'til lunch time.

Take a stand on this, parents: Put a system in place where no member of your household will face the day on an empty stomach.

FOLLOW THROUGH WITH A GOOD LUNCH

What you put in your sons' or daughters' lunches can increase their chances of a healthy life style. Starting them off with well-balanced, nutritionally-packed lunches will form good habits and set in place a healthy attitude to food that will stay with them all their lives.

To change your children's eating habits for the better, do so gradually. For a mid-morning snack give them an apple instead of a biscuit or mix fresh strawberries or raspberries into a natural yoghurt. This will improve their teeth as well as their diet. Once they start eating healthy food, they will find sweet snacks over-sweet.

Lunch should provide one third of your children's nutritional requirements for the day and should be made up of breads - wholemeal, wholemeal and white mixed, brown finger rolls, brown scones, wholemeal pitta bread, toasted baps - thinly coated with whole or low fat butter.

FILLING SUGGESTIONS:

- Chopped tomato with sliced ham or cubed roast meats
- Tuna fish and sliced celery with mayonnaise
- Turkey sliced with coleslaw
- Ham and cheese with coleslaw
- Tinned or fresh salmon with cucumber
- Corned beef with sliced tomato, egg and onion.

DRINKS:

- A flask of home-made soup.
- Unsweetened fruit juice.
- Milk, yoghurt drinks, and flavoured milk.

- A banana, apple, orange, etc. will bring your child's mid-day meal to a successful and healthy end.

If a biscuit or sweet bar is required, give them some fruit scones, muesli buns, honey tea bread (recipe p.100), or fruit slice. These have nutritional value as well as being good satisfying fillers. Make them at the weekend with the children and show them the joys of baking and they will appreciate them all the more. The comforting smell of baking is worth all the trouble!

Making
a Bowl of
SOUP

I am a product of Rockwell Catering School, now sadly closed, where for 3 years I had the opportunity of working with and studying under a German chef Franz Knoblough, a man who knew the meaning of flavour and where it came from. My publisher tells me that people are slow to respond when told to make their own stock and I am saddened by this.

On the next visit to your butcher ask him to chop some beef or lamb bones for you. Take them home, put in a heavy-based pot, add sufficient cold water to cover, and bring to the boil. Discard this liquid which may contain a lot of fat, and wash bones off in cold water, now fill up again with cold water and bring to the boil.

Stock is a base foundation liquid and as such should not be seasoned with salt, but it is my opinion that the addition of a pinch at the start will help to break down the protective membrane on the bone, as well as help to bring the scum to the top.

During the slow boiling process, some bay leaf, fresh herbs as well as a combination of carrot, celery and onion may be added to lend more flavour. Chicken or turkey stock is cooked in 90 minutes, but lamb or beef bones take a lot longer. When the stock is ready, strain and freeze in containers for later use.

Alternatively, roast the bones for about 1 hour and then boil with vegetables and herbs. This makes a brown stock.

Armed with a basic stock you can now confidently start to produce some truly memorable, hearty, economical dishes. Remember also if you would like your stock to have a really concentrated flavour, reduce it down to half its original quantity. You can fortify the flavour with a glass or two of red wine for special occasions. For fish stock see page 102.

Allow 10fl oz ($^1/_2$ pint) soup per person.

In a heavy saucepan, melt 15g ($^1/_2$oz) butter or 1 tablespoon sunflower oil, on a low heat.

Add 60g (2oz) each diced onions, diced celery and leek. Cover and cook slowly (sweat) for 4 minutes; do not allow to colour.

If you want a particular vegetable soup, just add 240g (8oz) of your chosen vegetable, chopped small and again sweat for a further 5 minutes. Add a bay leaf and any fresh herbs of your choice. Next, with the pan off the heat, add 1$^1/_4$ litres (2pts) stock, return to the boil and simmer for 20 to 40 minutes, depending on the ingredients involved. During cooking, remove scum that will rise as it forms. When all ingredients are soft, allow to cool for at least 1 hour, liquidise, taste and adjust seasoning if ncessary. Soups allowed to stand off the heat for a period of time before service will be enhanced in flavour, and just need to be reheated before serving.

Before serving, return to the boil and add a spoon of fresh cream.

Serve this with your own home made brown bread (page 102) and you are serving a meal of 100% goodness.

Make a turnip or parsnip soup in this way when these vegetables are in season, but just before adding the stock, put in 1 heaped teaspoon curry powder. Stir and cook over a very gentle heat for 2 to 3 minutes. Add stock and when the soup is ready to liquidise, a tablespoon of chutney will make a lovely addition to the finished product.

CELERY AND APPLE 'NO SWEAT' SOUP

Serves 4

1.25 litres (2 pints) good quality chicken or turkey stock
300g (10oz) chopped celery
1 medium cooking apple, washed and cored, but not peeled
30g (1oz) chopped onion
1 bayleaf
1 teasp fresh herbs or ½ teasp Herbes de Provence
2 rashers streaky bacon, diced.

✓ Bring stock to the boil in a heavy-based saucepan.

✓ Add chopped onion, bacon, celery, apple, bayleaf and herbs.

✓ Cover and simmer for 40 mins. Allow to cool, then liquidise.

✓ Return to acceptable eating temperature. A little pouring cream may be added for colour.

Serve with melba toast or thinly sliced brown bread.

This is an easy 'no sweat' soup. Everything goes in together and the blend of flavours is a marriage made in Heaven. You will find Herbes de Provence in the Schwartz range.

NETTLE SOUP

Serves 4

1 onion
15g (½oz) butter
1 bunch young nettles
Salt and pepper
1 litre (1.75 pints) chicken stock
1 large potato, chopped
1 stick celery, diced

✓ Pick the nettles with rubber gloves on and wear the gloves while washing and drying them.

✓ Sweat the onion, celery and potato in butter for 10 minutes, add the nettles, and cook until glossy.

✓ Add stock and cook for 20 minutes, cool and liquidise.

✓ Allow to stand overnight if possible in a very cold place to enhance the flavour.

✓ Reheat, add a little cream and serve immediately.

CARROT AND CORIANDER SOUP

Serves 4

1kg (2.2lb) carrots, diced

1.25 litres(2 pints) vegetable stock

500g (1lb) onions, diced

3 tbsps sunflower oil

Seasoning

1$\frac{1}{2}$ dessertsp crushed coriander seeds

✓ Heat the oil in a saucepan and add the finely diced onions.

✓ Sweat, covered with greaseproof paper for 5-8 minutes until soft.

✓ Add in the diced carrots and coriander and cook for a further 5 minutes.

✓ Add in the stock (a stock cube may be used if preferred).

✓ Bring to the boil and cook until the vegetables are soft.

✓ Season with salt and pepper and liquidise.

✓ Sieve to remove coriander seeds. Serve hot.

ICED, ROASTED TOMATO SOUP

Serves 4

4 medium onions, washed, unpeeled and halved

1 bulb garlic, split into cloves, unpeeled

1kg vine tomatoes, washed, halved and deseeded

1 tbsp good quality tomato pureé

1 teasp sugar

1 tbsp olive oil

1 fresh grapefruit, peeled and segmented

2 tbsps dry sherry

400ml stock

Salt and pepper

✓ Preheat the oven to gas 6; 200C; 400F.

✓ Place onions, garlic and tomatoes on a preheated roasting tin and add oil, sugar and seasoning.

✓ Toss together and roast for 30 minutes.

✓ When the vegetables are roasted, allow to cool completely.

✓ Peel onion and garlic.

✓ Combine stock, vegetables, tomato pureé, sherry and grapefruit. Liquidise and strain.

✓ Chill for 4-6 hours before service. Freshly ground black pepper and tabasco sauce can be served on the side.

SMOKED FISH CHOWDER

Serves 4-6

240g (8oz) smoked cod or haddock, cut in small cubes
1 stick celery, diced
1 carrot, diced
1 medium onion, diced
2 medium potatoes diced
1 leek, sliced
15g (1/2oz) butter or sunflower oil
15g (1/2oz) carrageen
300ml (10fl oz) milk
1 teasp tomato purée
600ml (20fl oz) fish stock (p.103)
Chopped parsley
Pinch black pepper
Cream

✓ Place prepared vegetables into a heavy-based saucepan with butter or oil and cover with a lid or greaseproof paper to sweat over low heat for 5 minutes.

✓ Add tomato purée, a teaspoon freshly chopped parsley and some freshly ground black pepper

✓ Add milk and fish stock, and return to a gentle boil.

✓ Add carrageen moss and turn heat down to simmer very gently for 10 mins.

✓ Add fish and simmer gently for about 7 minutes.

✓ Fresh cream added before serving will give this a rich texture.

✓ Serve immediately, in large bowls with crusty French stick, garlic bread or home made brown bread.

This is a meal in itself and can also use almost any type of unsmoked fish successfully. A few cubes of smoked bacon may be added with unsmoked fish to achieve the best of flavour.

Food for the gods, stand back and wait for the applause.

Vegetable Dishes & Salads

We are all aware of heart disease, cancer, diabetes, osteoporosis - they are common conditions in our society, but what causes them? Diet alone is not at fault but contributes, as do genetic environmental and various other factors.

In Ireland, UK and USA, fresh fruit and vegetable consumption is seriously out of line with Mediterranean statistics, and it is an established fact that eating raw as well as correctly cooked vegetables and fruit, can help in the prevention of many ailments. It is the duty of all of us who cook for a living, or feed our families, to remember this when compiling our weekly shopping list/menus. Let us then introduce a vegetarian day in every seven, and take it from there.

I am well aware of the up-hill struggle that lies before you to introduce this concept on to the domestic table, but believe me, you will succeed. You will be rewarded for your endurance in no time at all, with your children tucking into a vegetable-only main meal at least once a week.

Exercise a little care in the everyday cooking of vegetables, and please remember that the two greatest enemies of vegetables are water and heat. The least exposure to those elements, the better. Every time you add water and heat to cook vegetables, you destroy the valuable minerals and vitamins without even knowing it.

It is recommended that we eat at least 4 servings of fruit and vegetables each day, yet you may still not be getting all the goodness you think. Boiling green vegetables loses 50% of the vitamin C content, vitamins and minerals are unstable and soluble in water. To make the most of vegetables:

✓ never buy vegetables in bulk
✓ store in your fridge or on an open rack
✓ always remove vegetables from plastic bags
✓ scrub rather than peel – much of the goodness lies
   just underneath the skin.

- ✓ do not soak vegetables in water as vitamin loss will occur
- ✓ use a bare minimum of liquid when cooking, as nutrients from the vegetables dissolve in water.
- ✓ do not throw out water left over from cooking but use for stocks for soups etc.
- ✓ always use boiling water when cooking vegetables.
- ✓ salt should not be added before or during cooking vegetables as it draws out nutrients.
- ✓ never overcook vegetables
- ✓ when you think boiling potatoes need 'just a few more minutes', take off and strain immediately, allow to stand for a few minutes and they will finish cooking to perfection.

Pressure cooking is a good idea because very little water is used and no oxidation occurs. Different vegetables cook at different rates, so check the chart with the pressure cooker.

Steaming is my personal favourite way to cook vegetables. Vegetables are placed in a perforated steamer over a saucepan with a little boiling water and cooked for slightly longer than you would for boiling. Steamed vegetables retain almost all vitamins and minerals.

Stir-frying. Diverse colours and textures of vegetables are used here. Prepare close to the time required, and fry for 7-10 minutes in good quality oil. If you don't have a wok, don't worry, a good quality frying pan will do.

POTATO FRUIT PANCAKES

Serves 3-4

3 large potatoes
1 egg yolk
$1/_2$ teacup sifted flour
$3/_4$ teacup cottage
cheese, drained and
sieved
1 teasp salt
3 pears, peaches or
apples
4 tbsps
polyunsaturated oil

✓ Cook the potatoes in their skins until tender.

✓ Drain, peel and mash until smooth.

✓ Beat in the egg yolk, flour, salt and cottage
cheese.

✓ Peel and slice the fruit thinly.

✓ Grease 20 cm (9") skillet (with ovenproof
handle), or baking dish, with oil using a pastry
brush.

✓ Arrange the fruit in it and pour over the potato
mixture.

✓ Bake in the oven at Gas 5; 190C; 375F for
20 minutes, or until browned. Cut into wedges
and serve hot.

These are a particularly good accompaniment to
duck or meat dishes as well as a tasty supper
and lunch treat.

1 POT VEGETABLE MEAL

1 large red, green and yellow pepper, de-seeded and chopped
4 sticks celery, washed and chopped
2 medium carrots - skin removed and cut in finger sized pieces
1 medium onion, sliced
1 large parsnip, peeled and roughly chopped
2 leeks, washed and cut in 2.5cm (1") lengths
6 small potatoes, peeled and quartered
$1/_2$ teasp Herbes de Provence or bunch fresh seasonal herbs
1 teasp arrowroot (optional)
Freshly chopped parsley
Water
Salt & pepper

Additions:
Broccoli and Cauliflower florets are also ideal for this dish, cook on top, over potatoes.

◁ Cover base of pot with a layer of chopped celery, then a layer of carrot, then leek followed by parsnip, onion, red, green and yellow peppers and finish off with quartered potatoes.

◁ Sprinkle with herbs, freshly ground black pepper, a little salt, and a knob of butter.

◁ Pour over 4 tablespoons water, cover with tightly fitting lid and heat.

◁ When boiling point has been reached, reduce heat and allow to cook for 10 minutes.

Serve immediately, or, for slightly thicker sauce, strain juices into a small saucepan. Mix 1 teaspoon of arrowroot powder with a little cold milk, add to juices and return to the boil for 1 minute. Sprinkle a little freshly chopped parsley over individual portions.

This is one of my all-time favourites which could not be more simple.
A good no-sweat recipe

VEGETABLE LASAGNE

Serves 4-5

1kg/2.2lb. prepared
mixed vegetables,
roughly chopped (e.g.
onions, potatoes,
carrots, leeks,
parsnips, red and
green peppers)
1 clove garlic
400g (14oz) tinned
tomatoes
4 tbsps tomato purée
5fl oz (¹/₄ pt) hot stock

60g (2oz) plain flour
60g (2oz) butter
20fl oz (1pt) milk
12 sheets ready-cook
lasagne
2 tbsps grated cheese
Pinch salt and pepper

✓ Empty tinned tomatoes into a saucepan.

✓ Add the garlic, prepared vegetables, tomato
purée and seasoning.

✓ Cover and simmer for 15-20 minutes until
vegetables are soft.

✓ Stir in the boiling stock.

✓ Make a white sauce by melting the butter,
adding the flour and stirring for 1 minute. Add
the milk a splash at a time to make creamy
mixture, then add seasoning.

✓ Place a layer of the vegetables in the bottom
of an ovenproof dish.

✓ Top with 4 sheets of lasagne.

✓ Repeat the layers, ending with a layer of
lasagne.

✓ Pour over the white sauce and top with
grated cheese.

✓ Cook at Gas 6; 200C; 400F on the middle
shelf for approximately 35-40 minutes until the
lasagne is tender and the top golden brown.

This is a simple dish which uses any mixture of
seasonal vegetables layered with pasta to make
a complete meal. Frozen vegetables may also be
used. This dish can be frozen in segments and
used as needed. Omit the garlic if planning to
freeze it.

VEGETABLE CRUMBLE

1 medium red, green
and yellow pepper
240g (8oz) sweetcorn
1 medium onion, diced
1 large courgette, diced
1 large parsnip, diced
1 large carrot, diced
Large handful
mushrooms, sliced
1 teasp freshly-
chopped parsley
1 bay leaf
1 large potato, peeled
and diced

SAUCE:
30g (1oz) butter
30g (1oz) flour
900ml (1½ pt) low-fat
milk
2 tbsps Cheddar
cheese, grated

TOPPING:
240g (8oz) wholemeal
breadcrumbs
60g (2oz) peanuts (in
liquidiser for 5 seconds
or crushed with a
rolling pin)
¼ teasp mixed spices
1 tbsp currants
120g (4oz) melted
butter

✓ Place all vegetables in a saucepan, cover
with water and simmer for 4 minutes.

✓ Bring milk to the boil with bay leaf.

✓ In another saucepan melt butter, take off the
heat and add flour, stirring well. Return to a
low heat and cook for 1 minute, stirring all the
time. Slowly add milk minus the bay leaf and
cook for 3 minutes. Cool, add grated cheese
and salt and pepper to taste.

✓ Strain blanched vegetables and place in a
large ovenproof dish.

✓ Pour over sauce and sprinkle with freshly
chopped parsley.

✓ Combine wholemeal breadcrumbs, peanuts,
spice, currants and melted butter and spread
over vegetables.

✓ Bake for 40 minutes at Gas 5; 190C; 375F

CAULIFLOWER & BLUE CHEESE FLAN

Serves 6

PASTRY:
180g (6oz) plain flour
90g (3oz) butter/margarine
30g (1oz) shortening/lard (cooking fat)
2 tablesp cold water
Pinch salt

FILLING:
480g (1lb) prepared cauliflower florets
120g (4oz) blue cheese
30g (1oz) cheddar cheese, grated

ONION SAUCE:
30g (1oz) butter
1 onion, peeled and chopped
2 level tablesp flour
250ml (8fl oz) milk
Salt and black pepper

✓ Sieve flour and salt into a bowl.

✓ Rub in butter and shortening until mixture resembles fine breadcrumbs.

✓ Mix to a stiff paste with cold water.

✓ Roll out on a lightly-floured board and use to line a 23cm/9 inch flan ring.

✓ Prick the bottom of the pastry and line with greaseproof paper. Pour dried beans or lentils on top to keep paper down while cooking and place in oven. This is known as baking blind.

✓ Bake for 5 minutes at Gas 7; 220C; 425F. Remove from oven.

✓ Reduce oven temperature to Gas 5; 190C; 375F.

✓ Cook cauliflower in boiling, salted water until tender. Drain.

✓ Melt butter, add onion and cook slowly for 5 minutes.

✓ Add flour and cook gently for 1 minute, stirring.

✓ Remove pan from heat and gradually stir in the milk.

✓ Bring to the boil and continue to cook, stirring until the sauce thickens. Season.

✓ Sprinkle blue cheese over the base of flan case.

✓ Arrange cauliflower on top, pour over the onion sauce and sprinkle with the Cheddar cheese.

✓ Bake for about 30 minutes until golden and bubbling.
Serve hot.

LAYERED POTATO AND BACON CAKE

Serves 4

720g (1½lb) potatoes
480g (1lb) thick-cut
rindless, smoked
bacon, chopped
210g (7oz) mature
Cheddar cheese,
grated
2 tbsps snipped chives
Salt and freshly ground
black pepper
300ml (10fl oz) cream
2 medium eggs, beaten

✓ Preheat oven to Gas 6; 200C; 400F.

✓ Boil potatoes for about 5 minutes.

✓ Drain and leave until cool enough to handle, then peel and slice as thinly as possible.

✓ Cook the bacon in its own fat in a pan for 10 minutes or until crisp.

✓ In an ovenproof dish, layer potatoes, bacon and cheese, sprinkling with chives, salt and pepper as you do so. Finish with a cheese layer.

✓ Whisk cream with eggs and pour over.

Bake for 30-35 minutes or until the potatoes are cooked and the mixture is bubbling.

RATATOUILLE

Serves 4

1 aubergine, topped, tailed and sliced
Salt for sprinkling
1-2 tbsps olive oil or extra virgin olive oil
1 medium onion, peeled and sliced
2 courgettes, topped, tailed and sliced
1 large clove garlic, peeled and crushed
1 red pepper, sliced and diced
400g (14oz) tinned chopped tomatoes
Freshly ground black pepper
1 tbsp freshly chopped parsley

To garnish
Few sprigs flat leaf parsley

✓ Arrange the aubergine slices on a large plate and sprinkle with salt.

✓ Leave to stand for 30 minutes to draw any bitter juices. This is known as to de-gorge. Rinse thoroughly in cold water to remove the salt and dry on kitchen towel.

✓ Heat the olive oil in a large saucepan, add the onion and aubergine and toss around gently (sauté) for 5 minutes until softened.

✓ Add courgettes, garlic and peppers to the pan and fry for another 5 minutes

✓ Stir in the chopped tomatoes, pepper and parsley and leave to simmer for a further 15 minutes.

✓ Transfer to a warmed serving dish, garnish with parsley sprigs and serve immediately with crusty or Italian style bread.

HONEY-BRAISED RED CABBAGE

Serves 4

30ml (2 tbsps) oil
450g (1lb) red cabbage
1 large onion, sliced
1 stalk celery, sliced
Salt and freshly ground
black pepper
45ml (3 tbsps) clear
honey
30ml (2 tbsps) water
Pinch ground nutmeg
Pinch ground
cinnamon
2 medium cooking
apples, peeled and
thickly sliced
45ml (3 tbsps) cider
vinegar
150ml (5fl oz) red wine

◁ Heat oil in a fairly deep frying-pan or skillet. Add cabbage, onion and celery and season to taste.

◁ Cook, stirring, for 2-3 minutes then stir in honey, water and spices and continue to cook until mixture boils.

◁ Cover pan, reduce the heat and simmer for 5-15 minutes, depending on how tender you want the cabbage: after 5 minutes the vegetables will still be very crunchy, after 15 minutes they will be cooked enough to give a very soft result.

◁ Stir apples, cider vinegar and wine into cabbage and cook, uncovered, stirring, until most of the liquid has evaporated to leave a moist glaze on the cabbage (approx 4 minutes).

HOT BEETROOT & APPLE WITH SOUR CREAM AND CHIVES

Serves 6

2 large beetroots
2 eating apples
30g (1oz) butter
Salt & pepper
8 tbsps sour cream, fromage frais or Greek yoghurt, strained
2 tbsps fresh chives or spring onion, chopped

To serve:
6 slices bread with crusts removed
or 30g (1oz) breadcrumbs

✓ Bake beetroot whole and unpeeled for 60-90 minutes in the oven at Gas 2; 150C; 300F or boil or steam for 30-60 minutes.

✓ Allow to cool and cut into 5 mm (¹/₄ inch) slices and then halves.

✓ Quarter apples and core, but do not peel.

✓ Slice to same thickness of beetroot and arrange overlapping in a buttered ovenproof dish

✓ Season well and dot with butter.

✓ Cover with foil and bake at Gas 6; 200C; 400F for 20-30 minutes.

✓ Mix cream with chives.

✓ To serve as first course, cut bread into triangles and fry in butter, or toast until golden. Serve toast tucked around edges of dish.

✓ To serve as side-dish, fry or grill breadcrumbs until brown and sprinkle on top.

✓ Spoon cream down centre of dish to finish.

CARROT AND RICE MOULDS

Serves 6

240g (8oz) carrots
2 eggs
1 tbsp double cream
Lemon juice
Salt & pepper
Sprig tarragon
60g (2oz) rice
1 head lettuce
Tarragon to decorate

▽ Slice and cook carrots until tender.

▽ Drain and place in blender with eggs, cream, a squeeze of lemon juice, salt, pepper and tarragon.

▽ Cook rice, drain and stir into carrot mixture.

▽ Place 16 untorn lettuce leaves into a pot of salted, boiling water, return to boil for 10 seconds and remove lettuce.

▽ Rinse in cold water and drain.

▽ Brush 6 ramekin dishes or dariole moulds (ovenproof cups may be used) with oil and line with one or two lettuce leaves.

▽ Fill moulds with carrot mixture and fold overhanging lettuce on top.

▽ Cover each with foil and stand in roasting dish half filled with boiling water (bain marie).

▽ Bake at Gas 5; 190C; 375F for 15 minutes

▽ Turn out onto individual plates and decorate with fresh tarragon leaves.

Any combination of vegetables may be used in this simple but effective recipe. Try celeriac, peas, broad beans, instead of carrot.

CARROT MATCHSTICKS

Serves 4

480g (1lb) carrots
1 level teasp sugar
Pinch salt and black
pepper
1 teasp butter

✓ Scrub or lightly peel the carrots, then cut carrot into matchstick pieces.

✓ Place in a saucepan.

✓ Add rest of ingredients and cover with a lid.

✓ Bring to the boil, then reduce the heat and cook for 5 minutes.

✓ Remove lid and cook for 1 minute more to allow water evaporate. The final result will be shiny glazed, slightly firm carrots which have retained their natural sweetness.

WARM SALAD WITH BACON AND PINEAPPLE

Serves 4

480g (1lb) back bacon,
rinded and cut in strips
240g (8oz) chopped
pineapple
Vinaigrette dressing or
mustard and honey
dressing (see page 31)
Freshly ground black
pepper
Selection lettuces

✓ Wash and tear lettuce in pieces. Store for at least 1 hour in the fridge to refresh.

✓ Before serving, toss in dressing and arrange lettuce in the centre of a large white plate.

✓ Fry bacon in a very hot pan until golden brown. Add chopped pineapple and stir.

✓ Sprinkle bacon and pineapple over lettuce and serve immediately.

GRILLED VEGETABLE SALAD

Serves 4-6

120g (4oz) Mozzarella cheese, cubed
Mustard and Honey dressing
480g (1lb) plum tomatoes,chopped
2 small aubergines
Rock salt and black pepper
Olive oil for drizzling
1 red pepper
1 yellow pepper
240g (8oz) baby or small courgettes

✓ Mix Mozzarella and tomatoes with dressing and allow to marinate.

✓ Thinly slice aubergines, place on a baking sheet, season and drizzle with olive oil. Place under a pre-heated grill until crisp.

✓ Repeat process, cutting the peppers into chunks and slicing the courgettes lengthways. Add grilled vegetables to Mozzarella and tomato and serve immediately.

MUSTARD & HONEY SALAD DRESSING

30ml (2 tbsps) clear honey
30ml (2 tbsps) balsamic vinegar
45ml (3 tbsps) olive oil
30ml (2 tbsps) torn basil leaves(optional)
1 tbsp (15ml) clear honey
1 tbsp (15ml) Dijon mustard
Pinch salt
2 tbsps (30ml) lemon juice
4 tbsps (6ml) sunflower oil or a mixture sunflower and olive oils

✓ Shake all ingredients together in a lidded jar.

✓ Store in a cool place or refrigerate.

31

FRANK'S BASICS: MAYONNAISE

When making mayonnaise, the freshness of eggs is very important.

2 egg yolks (Size 3)
¼ teasp salt
Pinch white pepper
300ml (½ pt) sunflower oil
300 ml (½ pt) extra virgin olive oil
1 tbsp (15ml) Dijon mustard
Juice 1 lemon
2 tbsps boiled water, cooled slightly

☑ Separate the eggs and put the yolks into a liquidiser or bowl with the salt and pepper.

☑ At full speed, beat the yolks and begin adding the sunflower oil a few drops at a time, until it starts to thicken.

☑ Start to pour the oil in a thin stream until all the sunflower oil is incorporated. The mixture will now be very thick.

☑ Beat in the mustard and half the lemon juice then the olive oil. If still too thick, add the rest of the lemon juice and some boiled water, a tablespoon at a time. When you have incorporated all the oil, taste and add more salt and pepper if needed. The final consistency should be that of double cream.

Leftover egg-whites have numerous uses, including meringues, Pavlova and macaroon biscuits. They can also be used to clarify the impurities out of stock. The stock is heated and the egg white dropped in and boiled for a few minutes. The sediment is attracted to the egg white which is removed with a slotted spoon and discarded to give a perfect clear stock suitable for consommé and making aspic.

Warm Salad with
Bacon and Pineapple

Poached Fillet of Lemon Sole
with Mussel Stuffing and Tomato Sauce

EGGCETERA

A PERFECT BOILED EGG

A small heavy-based saucepan is best with enough water to completely submerge the egg. A pinch of salt in the water will help keep the egg intact, should a crack occur. Eggs should always be at room temperature prior to cooking and not straight out of the 'fridge. When water has reached the boil, remove saucepan from heat, gently lower egg into water and only then return to a gentle boil. Three minutes from the moment the egg comes to the boil, your softly cooked egg is ready.

For hard-boiled eggs, continue cooking for another three minutes. When cooked, allow water to drain off and let the cold tap run on the eggs for three to four minutes to prevent discolouration.

PERFECT POACHED EGGS

I love poached eggs, and was instructed in the production of the perfect specimen by a 9 year-old boy scout. His method was beautifully simple, although you must cook only 1 egg at a time: A small container of lightly salted boiling water is needed to which you add 1 teaspoon of lemon juice or vinegar. This addition of acid will keep the white of the egg intact and the presentation of the egg like a white pillow.

Break the egg onto a saucer and with a large spoon, agitate the water and slide the egg from the saucer into this. Maintain the liquid at just under boiling for 3 minutes and there is your perfectly poached egg.

PERFECT SCRAMBLED EGGS

Contrary to what you may have read before, when making scrambled eggs no form of liquid should be added.

For supreme perfection, break up 2 eggs with a fork (never use an egg-beater or whisk). Add salt and pepper to taste and a knob of butter. Cook this in a well-buttered small heavy-based pot, dislodging all the time with a wooden spoon (note I didn't say stirring as this is too severe – keep it light). The eggs should be still runny before turning out onto some freshly made toast. Smoked salmon added as a garnish is a fashionable addition.

PERFECT OMELETTES

There are so many fillings and garnishes that can be used in omelettes that I could write about them all day.

My favourite omelette consists of :

3 eggs, broken up with a fork (do not beat), 1 tablespoon grated cheese, 1 medium cold cooked potato (peeled and diced) which should be tossed in butter with freshly chopped parsley for 2 minutes over heat.

Pour eggs on to a well-greased hot frying pan and immediately tilt the pan from side to side to draw in the congealed egg from the sides to the centre. At 90 seconds, your omelette is ready for the filling: spoon heated diced potato into the centre and sprinkle with a tablespoon of grated cheddar cheese, before folding to one side of the pan and serving immediately.

PERFECT FRIED EGGS

For the ultimate fried egg, submerge completely in clear fat for three minutes. You may consider this to be an over-exposure to fat, and I agree, but it does produce a beautiful egg.

PERFECT EGGS EN COCOTTE

As a starter for a dinner party, eggs come into their own with a variety of flavours to enhance them. These are cooked individually in ramekins or ovenproof cups and look attractive served on saucers or large plates.

Butter a small ovenproof dish or ramekin and spoon 1 tablespoon cream into it. Break 2 eggs, one at a time, into a saucer and slide eggs from it into ramekin. Scatter 1 dessertspoon of finely chopped mushrooms and some chopped parsley over top, season with salt and pepper and cover with foil. Place ramekin in a roasting dish with boiling water which comes half way up the dishes (bain marie) and cook on top of the stove or in oven until egg whites are set (approx. 5-6 minutes)

pasta

Like wine, we are very steadily discovering the many different pastas now on offer. It is my opinion that making ones own pasta is for the purist, not the busy home cook. These recipes make the best of the convenience of pasta, with simple and satisfying sauces.

Cook the pasta according to instructions on the packet, allowing about 60g (2oz) uncooked pasta per portion and remembering that the Italians manage to keep their pasta firm by using plenty of salt in the cooking water. Drain and toss with a knob of butter or a drizzle of olive oil. Pile portions of the pasta into individual serving dishes and grate Parmesan cheese and a little sea salt. Serve hot.

BOLOGNESE STYLE PASTA SAUCE

Serves 5

**480g (1lb) minced beef
(have it minced in your
presence)
1 tbsp (15ml) sunflower
oil
60g (2oz) finely diced
onion
Few cloves garlic,
crushed
480g (1lb) tin tomatoes
or 2 tbsps tomato
purée
1 teasp parsley
(optional)
½ teasp ground
nutmeg (optional)
300ml (10fl oz) beef
stock**

✓ Fry the mince briskly and thoroughly in the heated oil.

✓ Add the onion and garlic and turn down heat to allow to cook until wilted.

✓ Add tomatoes or purée, parsley and nutmeg.

✓ Add enough stock to cover the meat and allow to bubble gently for 20 minutes. The sauce is ready to eat and can be cooled and reheated later. The flavour improves with time.

BASIC TOMATO SAUCE FOR PASTA

Serves 4-6

1kg (2.2lb) ripe
tomatoes (or 2 tins)
2 tbsps
olive/sunflower/
grapeseed oil
1 clove garlic
1 onion
1 carrot
1 celery stick or
handful mushrooms,
sliced
1 teasp sugar
$\frac{1}{2}$ teasp oregano or
dried basil (optional)
Pinch salt and freshly
ground black pepper
Chopped herbs e.g.
thyme, rosemary,
parsley
Olives (optional)
Cheese and cream
(optional)

✓ Scald the tomatoes, peel, de-seed and chop.

✓ Heat oil in a saucepan, add garlic and chopped onion and sauté until golden.

✓ Add carrot and celery, then tomatoes and fresh herbs.

✓ Simmer at a gentle heat for 15 mins.

✓ If using basil add at this stage and simmer for a further 5 minutes.

✓ Season with salt and freshly ground black pepper.

✓ Liquidise and strain before serving.

✓ Stir in grated cheese and cream and/or olives. Additional milk, cream or yoghurt may be added to correct consistency.

This is a simple sauce which is good with beef, chicken, fish and any type of vegetables added. The option to use celery or mushroom will give different texture and flavour. The mushrooms make a slightly heavier sauce.

LEMON AND DILL CREAM

Serves 2

✓ Gently heat 300 ml (10 fl oz) cream in a saucepan.

✓ When just about to bubble, stir in grated rind 1 lemon and 2 tbsps freshly chopped dill, a few twists freshly ground black pepper completes this sauce.

This is particularly good with penne pasta or tagliatelle. Add chopped smoked salmon for a special treat just before serving.

Lemon & Dill seasoning (you will find this in the Schwartz range) can substitute for fresh herbs

SPINACH AND PINE NUT SAUCE FOR PASTA

✓ Heat 3 tablespoons groundnut oil in a frying pan

✓ Add 2 chopped spring onions and 2 chopped garlic cloves and cook until soft.

✓ Trim stalks 240g (8oz) spinach and add to pan with just a pinch of salt, pepper and grated nutmeg.

✓ When wilted, blend until smooth, or chop finely.

✓ Sprinkle in 60g (2oz) toasted pine nuts before serving hot. (Serves 4)

BUTTER AND HERB SAUCE FOR PASTA

✓ Melt 120g (4oz) butter, put into liquidiser with a small bunch of parsley minus stalks, and snipped chives.

✓ Whizz until all herbs are chopped. (Serves 4)

Serve immediately.

fish

MAKE MORE OF FISH

As a country surrounded by water, with fish ranked in the top 5 of our export industries, is it not amazing that the Irish eat surprisingly little fish? A legacy, I feel, of bygone days when fish was only offered on Fridays, as Penance Food, never the meal to be looked forward to.

Yet, correctly cooked, fish must be by far and away the most invaluable health-giving source of food that you can put on your daily table. Fish we are told, particularly the cheaper varieties, is very high in the Omega 3 fatty acids, which help to break down cholesterol formation in the blood stream, thereby reducing the risk of heart attack.

In my little restaurant on Inis Meáin, I sell vast quantities of freshly-caught pollack, cooked in numerous ways, to the sizeable amount of contented visitors that make their way there each year. Let me say at the outset, pollack is a beautiful fish if cooked simply and correctly on the day it is caught. But it has a very poor shelf life and does not react favourably to freezing.

Nearly every morning the young boys of the island, arrive at my kitchen door with the morning's catch. This I wash and fillet, and immediately set about making my daily requirement of fish stock, which in turn will form the basis of the day's seafood chowder.

Some of the filleted fish is simply dipped in seasoned flour then egg wash (1 egg, 1/2pt milk beaten together) and coated in my own homemade breadcrumbs. It should be allowed to stand for 30 minutes before deep-frying in hot oil or fat. I serve this with homemade tartare sauce and fresh salad for lunch. I make fresh mayonnaise every morning, it takes 5 minutes, and, quite apart from flavour, economically beats the socks off the bought product (see page 32 for recipe.)

It sometimes happens, as a result of bad weather, that a supply of fresh fish may not be available to you. On occasions such as this, why not use one of the many excellent types of smoked fish, which are cooked in the same way.

Never, ever, boil fish. If the flesh is over-exposed to constant boiling action, you will succeed in cooking out the essential oils or protein of the fish, and thereafter it is not worth eating. Poaching gently in a flavoured liquid gives a much better result.

Clearly a stock made from the bones of the fish you are about to cook is ideal. But most of us nowadays must rely on supermarkets as our suppliers of fresh fish, and the fish is often filleted and prepared at source long before it reaches the shop. A Court Bouillon is the best substitute. I have given a simple recipe on page 47 and a recipe for stock on page 103.

White sauce is a good accompaniment to poached fish. Make a simple white sauce using milk to poach the fish in and then add this to a roux (flour and butter paste, see recipe page 103).

When fish is cooked, strain the cooking liquid on to the roux and simmer gently for 5 mins. If the liquid used for cooking the fish is water-based add some milk or pouring cream to get a good creamy consistency.

Before pouring sauce over the fish to serve, add 15g (1oz) freshly grated Cheddar cheese, and for added effect sprinkle some cheese over the sauce, and flash under a hot grill for a minute or two.

SMOKED FISH & CREAM CHEESE PATÉ

Serves 10

480g (1lb) smoked fish, cooked and flaked
90g (3oz) cream cheese
90g (3oz) butter, softened
Pinch black pepper
Dash tabasco
2 tbsps (30ml) lemon juice
1 tbsp (15ml) cream, lightly whipped
1 tbsp (15ml) horseradish sauce

✓ Blend all ingredients together in a food processor.
✓ Fill moulds, teacups, ramekins and allow to chill.

CARRAGEEN AND MUSSEL SAUCE

Serves 10

1¼ litres (2 pints) well reduced fish stock
15g (½oz) carrageen, steeped in water for 1 hour
1 cup mussels, out of their shells
2 tbsps pouring cream

✓ Heat stock and cream in a saucepan and bring to a gentle boil.
✓ Add carrageen and simmer for 5 minutes.
✓ Strain.
✓ Add mussels and heat gently with the lid of the saucepan on.

Serve immediately.

FISH CAKES

480g (1lb) any white fish, filleted and skin removed.
300ml (10fl oz) court bouillon (see recipe p.47)
480g (1lb) potatoes boiled in their jackets and mashed.
60g (2oz) finely diced onion.
15g (¹/₂oz) butter.
1 teasp fresh parsley.
Pinch sea salt and white pepper
1 egg beaten with 300ml (10fl oz) milk
Fresh breadcrumbs (allow ¹/₂ slice bread per fish cake)
Oil & butter for frying

▽ Boil potatoes in their jackets, peel and mash immediately.

▽ Add butter, onion, pepper, salt and pepper

▽ Bring the court bouillon to the boil, and reducing the heat add the fish and poach very gently for 5 minutes.

▽ When cooked remove the fish immediately from the cooking liquid, otherwise it will absorb a lot of the water.

▽ Reserve cooking liquor.

▽ When cold, mix fish with potato.

▽ Coat your hands with flour, and mould mixture into 4 equal sized cakes.

▽ Dip in seasoned flour, then in a wash made with 1 egg with 300ml (10fl oz) milk

▽ Finish by coating with fresh breadcrumbs.

▽ Allow to stand for 30 mins.

▽ Heat oil and butter in frying pan

▽ Seal fish cakes on both sides until nicely browned, and finish off in a moderately hot oven for 20 minutes.

▽ Serve with carrageen and mussel sauce or a tartare sauce.

CRAB CAKES

Replace fish with 240g (8oz) cooked crab meat

STIR-FRIED PRAWNS

Serves 4

24-32 prawns, shelled and defrosted
400g cooked brown rice
2 tbsps honey
6 tbsps white wine vinegar
1 chilli finely chopped (optional)
100g cooked peas
A little oil

✓ Heat a little oil in a large frying pan or wok.

✓ Put prawns and chilli into the pan, cover and cook for 2-3 minutes, stirring occasionally.

✓ Add the honey and white wine vinegar, cook for 1 minute.

✓ Mix the cooked brown rice and peas in with the prawns and heat through.

Use any vinegar in this recipe but adjust the amount of honey to taste.
If using frozen peas, add them at the same time as the prawns.

TUNA WITH CRUSHED PEPPER

Serves 4

4 tuna steaks
Freshly milled or crushed peppercorns
A little oil

Serve with boiled potatoes and fresh garden vegetables.

✓ Sprinkle crushed peppercorns onto a plate.

✓ Press tuna steaks gently into the peppercorns.

✓ Add a dessertspoon of oil to the pan and heat through.

✓ Cook the tuna steaks in the pan. Turn once halfway through cooking time.

Tuna can also be grilled. It can be cooked from rare to well-done depending on individual tastes. The size of the tuna steak will dictate the cooking time. An average sized steak will take:
Well done – 8 minutes
Medium to well done – 6 minutes
Medium – 5 minutes
Medium to rare – 3-4 minutes
Rare – 2 minutes

FISH STROGANOFF

900g (2lb) firm white fish: angler, white pollock, eel or rock salmon, filleted and skinned.
2 onions, thinly sliced
240g (8oz) mushrooms, thinly sliced
Corn oil and butter
15g (1/₂oz) sieved flour
30ml (1fl oz) wine
Juice 1/₄ lemon
125ml (4fl oz) cream
Salt, pepper, sugar, chopped parsley

Serve with cooked long - grained rice

✓ Heat a little oil and butter in pan and cook onions and mushrooms until soft.

✓ Sprinkle on flour and stir well. Add wine and cream and allow to bubble for a few seconds. Add lemon juice.
Cut fish into strips and add to mixture.

✓ Cook gently for 3 minutes and serve immediately.

BASIC COURT BOUILLON

500ml (16fl oz) water.
1 slice lemon.
90g (3oz) combination chopped carrot, celery and onion
Pinch sea salt
Sprig parsley.

✓ Bring all ingredients to the boil, and simmer for 12 minutes, strain and use to poach fish.

For a special occasion, a dash of white wine may be added.

PORTUGUESE COD AND POTATOES

Serves 4-5

720g (1¹/₂lb) smoked
cod
1kg (2.2lb) potatoes
3 tbsps olive oil
2 large onions, sliced
1 clove garlic, chopped
20 black olives, stoned
Chopped parsley to
garnish

✓ Preheat oven to Gas 6; 200C; 400F.

✓ Place cod in saucepan with water to cover
and cook gently until fish will flake easily.

✓ Remove from water, discard skin and bones
and flake flesh with a fork.

✓ Peel potatoes and cook until just tender.

✓ Drain and cut into thick slices.

✓ Heat half the olive oil in a frying pan and
gently cook onions and garlic until soft but not
coloured.

✓ Brush baking dish with a little oil.

✓ Spread half the potato slices over bottom of
dish, cover with half the fish, onions and garlic
and olives, coarsely chopped. Repeat the
layers.

✓ Drizzle remaining olive oil over top and bake
for about 25 minutes. Garnish with remaining
olives and chopped parsley.
Serve with tomato or green salad.

This is the perfect all-in-one dish which tastes as
well cold as hot. Leftover potato may be used as
can any other thick unsmoked fish like monkfish
or thick fillets of whiting. Delicious salty anchovies
may be added if using unsmoked fish. For
emergency days a can of tuna makes it a
different but very satisfying dish.

48

POACHED FILLET OF LEMON SOLE WITH MUSSEL STUFFING AND TOMATO SAUCE

Serves 4

**4 180g (6oz) fillets
lemon sole
Fish stock (see page
103) or court bouillon
(page 47)**

**SAUCE:
30g (1oz) butter
30g (1oz) flour
2 tbsps tomato purée
900ml (1½ pt) fish
stock
1 teasp sugar**

**STUFFING:
90g (3oz) mussel meat
Freshly ground black
pepper
1 tbsp (15ml) whipped
cream
1 tbsp (15ml) Pernod
1 teasp lemon juice
1 egg yolk**

▽ Mix stuffing ingredients together.

▽ Place 1 tablespoon stuffing onto each fish and fold over.

▽ When required, poach in fish stock for 6-8 minutes.

▽ Meanwhile, in a small saucepan melt butter, add flour and cook for 1 minute, stirring. Add tomato purée and mix well.

▽ Add fish stock and sugar and cook for 3 minutes.

▽ Serve fish with sauce coating and remainder of sauce in sauce boat.

MONKFISH KEBABS

Monkfish has a firm, almost meaty flesh and a delicious flavour. Only the tail piece is used and is usually sold skinned, although it will still have a tough, clear membrane which needs to be removed before cooking. Buy a tail piece and remove the single thick bone running down the centre yourself, or buy prepared fillets. Monkfish is suitable for all types of cooking. Try pan-frying the fillets in butter with garlic and herbs or roasting the whole tail like a joint of meat. Or try these quick and easy kebabs.

◁ Marinate 360g (12oz) cubed monkfish in the juice and finely grated rind 1 lemon, 45ml (3 tbsps) virgin olive oil and a few fresh bay leaves.

◁ Thread the marinated fish onto 8 wooden skewers with lemon slices and large prawns (with tails still on) and grill for 8-10 mins until just cooked.

◁ Season with freshly ground black pepper and serve with a green salad.

FISHERMAN'S FLAN

Shortcrust Pastry see page 102

FILLING:
360g (12oz) smoked haddock or cod
300ml (10fl oz) milk
2 eggs, hard-boiled and quartered
30g (1oz) butter
30g (1oz) plain flour
Salt and black pepper
360g (12oz) mashed cooked potato
60g (2oz) Cheddar cheese, grated

☑ Make pastry case by lining a flan tin with shortcrust pastry and chill in 'fridge while making filling.

☑ Place fish in a saucepan with the milk, bring to the boil and simmer for 15 minutes.

☑ Strain the milk into a bowl and allow fish to cool enough to handle.

☑ Remove skin and bones from the fish and flake the flesh.

☑ Place fish in the pastry case.

☑ Arrange eggs over fish.

☑ In a saucepan, melt butter, add flour and cook gently for 1 minute, stirring. Remove from heat and gradually stir in the reserved milk. Bring to the boil and simmer over a gentle heat until sauce thickens, stirring well. Season to taste.

☑ Pour sauce into flan case.

☑ Pipe the potato across the top or spread and score with a fork.

☑ Sprinkle with cheese.

☑ Bake in a pre-heated oven Gas 5; 190C; 375F; for about 25 minutes.

Serve hot with a crisp green salad.

SEAFOOD PANCAKES

Serves 6

90g (3oz) flour
Pinch pepper and salt
1 egg
1 tbsp (15ml) oil or
melted butter
300ml (10fl oz) milk

✓ Sieve flour, salt and pepper into a bowl.
✓ Make a well in the centre flour and add egg and oil. Gradually add the milk beating all the time.
✓ Allow batter to rest for 1 hour if desired.

FISH FILLING

240g (8oz) cooked
shelled prawns
480g (1lb) cooked cod,
haddock or whiting

600ml (20fl oz) cheese
sauce
Pinch pepper and salt

✓ Flake fish into small pieces, add to cheese sauce with the prawns. Season with pepper and salt and heat thoroughly.
✓ Divide this mixture between pancakes and lay side by side in serving dish. Pour some cheese sauce over and place under grill to heat through and brown slightly.
✓ Serve hot with lemon wedges.

chicken

ROASTING POULTRY
======================

ROASTING POULTRY

Here are a few simple easy-to-follow hints that will enhance your poultry roast:

Never allow meat, especially poultry, to make direct contact with the roasting tin. If you don't have a trivet, use the tray from your grill pan. Put the bird sitting on this, and make sure the oven is at correct temperature before roast goes in.

Always, after washing inside and outside of bird, sprinkle inside of cavity with salt and pepper and some herbs of your choice. I find Schwartz Herbes de Provence to be excellent.

Do you or don't you stuff the chicken or turkey? My opinion is that it is perfectly in order to stuff the neck of a turkey, but on no account should you stuff the body cavity. It is advisable, however, to place half an onion, half an apple and an orange into the body cavity of large birds to prevent drying out the breast. Even small birds benefit from half an onion inside, along with a wedge of lemon. See recipe page 60.

Basting the bird during cooking is advisable to keep the flesh moist and tasty.

Always make a fresh gravy from the remains in the roasting tin when the bird is removed, scraping every bit of sediment.

Allow the roasted bird to stand for 20 minutes, covered with a warm damp cloth or foil before carving to allow the flesh to relax and make it easy to carve.

Make a fresh gravy in the roasting pan over a gentle heat on the cooker hob.

Remove most of the fat and then add a sprinkling of flour to mop up what is left. Brown gently, then add chicken stock made from the giblets. You may have to ask for giblets when buying the chicken as they are not always included. Use them with a carrot, stick of celery and an onion and boil in water for 30 minutes. For a slightly peppery gravy add a pinch of black and red pepper.

SIMPLE STOCK FROM FINISHED CARCASS OF CHICKEN

Put carcass of a cooked chicken into a saucepan and cover with water, bring to the boil and simmer for 50 minutes with some chopped vegetables, a bay leaf and a pinch of salt. Strained off, this will make a base foundation for a fresh soup.

Chicken legs represent great value. Ask your supplier to remove the bone to make a tasty feast for the family which can be varied by season. Fresh Tarragon is good in summer, as well as Rosemary which should be used sparingly. See recipes ahead for ideas with chicken legs. Do not be afraid to vary herbs and spices. Experiment with lemon instead of orange in the recipe on page 57 and use different types of mustards and chutneys to vary the final result in the recipes on page 56. You will find your family's favourites emerge as they become accustomed to the interesting variety which can be made with a simple adjustment to a recipe. However, follow the basic methods of roasting, poaching etc. carefully to minimise waste and maximise flavour.

CHICKEN LEG WITH CHUTNEY AND MUSTARD STUFFING, SERVED ON A BASIC GRAVY Serves 4

6 chicken legs
180g (6oz) whole-meal breadcrumbs
45g (1½oz) butter
30g (1oz) very finely diced onion
1 teasp Herbes de Provence
1 tbsp chutney
1 teasp mustard
Salt & pepper
to taste

✓ Flatten chicken legs by tapping with a rolling pin between two sheets of greaseproof paper.

✓ Season with freshly ground black pepper and salt.

✓ Make stuffing by frying onion in butter until soft. Add to breadcrumbs with herbs, chutney and mustard. Allow to cool.

✓ Place some of the stuffing on each piece of chicken and roll up.

✓ Wrap in greased tin foil.

✓ Cook in a moderate oven for 25 minutes.

✓ Allow to stand for 5 minutes, unwrap.

Serve with a sauce made from the roasted bones of the chicken legs boiled in 1 litre (1¾ pints) water and reduced to half the quantity. Add 1teaspoon of redcurrant jelly at the last minute for a light sweet flavour which compliments the chicken stuffing. Stuffing could also consist of 30g (1oz) wholemeal bread crumbs per leg, a little finely diced onion cooked in a knob of butter with 1 teaspoon prepared mustard mixed together.

CHICKEN DRUMSTICKS WITH SWEET SAUCE

✓ Bring some chicken drumsticks to the boil in lightly salted water, cook for 5 minutes, then remove from water and allow to cool.

✓ Reserve liquid for soup or another sauce.

✓ Coat in seasoned flour then egg wash (1 egg mixed with 300ml (10fl oz) milk). Pat firmly with breadcrumbs and stand for 20 minutes.

✓ Deep fry in hot oil for 4 minutes.

✓ Serve on a sauce of 1 tablespoon each of pineapple juice, tomato purée and brown vinegar brought to boil and allowed to simmer for 5 minutes.

CHICKEN THIGHS IN RED WINE

✓ Brown chicken thighs or drumsticks in a pot with a knob of butter and diced streaky bacon for 5 minutes.

✓ Add 1 teaspoon flour, 1 teaspoon tomato purée, a pinch Herbes de Provence.

✓ Mix well and cook for 2 minutes.

✓ Add a glass of red table wine and return to the boil.

✓ Add enough chicken stock to make a smooth sauce.

✓ Cook in a casserole in the oven at Gas 4; 180C; 350F for 20 minutes.

✓ Just before serving, take 30g (1oz) fresh mushrooms per person and quarter and toss them in butter to glaze. Add to dish for the last 5 minutes.

ORANGE GINGER CHICKEN

Serves 2

1 tbsp cornflour
Salt and pepper
240g (8oz) turkey/chicken breast
1 tablesp (15ml) olive oil
4 tbsps (60ml) concentrated orange juice
2 teasp wine/dry sherry
1 teasp brown sugar
1 lump stem ginger or ½inch/1cm fresh root ginger, peeled and very thinly sliced
4 peeled and sliced small potatoes
1 orange, peeled and sliced

✓ Mix the cornflour and seasoning together and sprinkle over the chicken.

✓ Sauté in olive oil until golden all over. Place in a small casserole dish.

✓ Mix the orange juice, wine/dry sherry and sugar together and pour over the top.

✓ Add slices of ginger, cover and bake at Gas 4; 180C; 350F, 30 minutes.

✓ Add the potatoes and orange, recover and continue cooking for about 45 minutes.

SATAY SAUCE FOR CHICKEN

1 medium onion, finely chopped
30ml (1fl oz) oil
1 teasp ground cumin
1 teasp curry powder
2 teasp Thai 7 spice seasoning/chilli powder
360g (12oz) crunchy peanut butter
30ml (1fl oz) tomato purée
45ml (1¹/₂fl oz) clear honey
45ml (1¹/₂fl oz) Branston Pickle
Water

✓ In a large pan fry the onion in oil until softened.

✓ Add the spices and cook for 1 minute.

✓ Mix in remaining ingredients and 375 ml (12 fl oz) water.

✓ Bring to the boil, stirring, then simmer gently until thickened and the peanut oil separates.

Satay sauce can be used for pork chops, chicken joints and vegetables. The marinade is useful for most barbecued meats. Try the Schwartz range for spices.

SPICY CHICKEN WING MARINADE

For 900g (2lb) chicken wings:
60ml (2fl oz) 4 tbsps sesame oil
60ml (2fl oz) 4 tbsps white wine vinegar
45ml (1½fl oz) 3 tbsps crunchy peanut butter
45ml (1½fl oz) 3 tbsps clear honey
30ml (1fl oz) 2 tbsps chilli sauce

☑ Whisk together marinade ingredients.

☑ Place chicken wings in a large container and pour over marinade

☑ Cover and refrigerate for as long as possible, preferably overnight

☑ Pre-heat oven to Gas 7; 220C; 425F, and bake chicken wings with marinade for 35-40 minutes, turning and basting frequently.

CIDER GLAZED CHICKEN

Serves 4

1 small onion, halved
1 lemon, quartered
1.35kg (3lb) oven-ready chicken
60ml (2fl oz) clear honey
1 clove garlic, crushed
2 teasp mustard powder
Salt and freshly ground black pepper
3 bay leaves
500ml (16fl oz) dry cider

✓ Pre-heat oven to Gas 5; 190C; 375F.

✓ Place the onion and lemon inside the body cavity of the chicken then transfer to a baking tin.

✓ Mix together honey, garlic and mustard with plenty of seasoning. Spread mixture over chicken and place bay leaves on top of the bird.

✓ Place in the oven and cook for 40 minutes.

✓ Warm the cider, then carefully pour it over chicken and continue to cook, uncovered, for a further 50-60 minutes. Baste chicken frequently during cooking and cover it loosely with foil if it becomes too dark.

✓ At the end of the cooking time, drain the liquid from the chicken and transfer it to a saucepan. Return the bird to the oven to keep hot.

✓ In a small pan bring the liquid to the boil, then boil, uncovered, until it is reduced by about three-quarters of its original quantity (10-15 minutes).

Place the chicken on a serving dish and pour over the glaze.

Meat &
Meat Dishes

Meat is one of the most important protein suppliers of all foods. Animal protein found in meat is especially used in the building and maintenance of the human body. The average protein content, although it differs from one sort of meat to another, amounts to about 20%, the fat content between 10% to 50%.

It is important to discuss with your butcher the most suitable cuts of meat for a particular dish. When making a casserole or stew, use stewing meat only. The slow protracted cooking of meat and sauce together will give a superb flavour. Ideally, cook at least 24 hours before needed, allowing to stand overnight in a cold room or refrigerator. Return to acceptable eating temperature when required.

Always remember that the advantage of casserole cooking is twofold, since you can cook vegetables and potatoes in the same oven thereby usefully reducing your energy bill at the same time.

Never throw away the bones. Make stock - see page 12.

When cooking casseroles or stews, cook double quantities and freeze one for another meal. It is advisable to thaw for 24 hours at room temperature before re-heating for use.

Supermarkets on an on-going basis have special offers on all meats on different weeks. Acquaint yourself with next week's offers and write your menu accordingly.

Meat without a little fat can be tasteless and dry. While lumps of fat in mince are not desirable, a little is recommended. Have meat minced in your presence unless you are very confident in your butcher.

Pork is real value for money, and careful consideration when buying brings a variety of inexpensive dishes to your table. When buying pork, always ensure the meat is fresh to get the best flavour.

The preparation of dishes using meat of older animals will take considerably longer to cook than the meat of the younger animal. Meat gets darker as it gets older, so judge cooking times accordingly.

Oxtail, liver, kidney, heart, tripe, collectively known as offal, are the most nutritious and good value foods which can feed a family. Over the last thirty years I have had many excellent meals, but one stands out. It was with German couple in Castletownberehaven, County Cork, who cooked it in their home. We started with lamb's kidneys, neatly diced and fried in butter with garlic, mushrooms and onion and finished off with a basic brown sauce to which a spoonful of port was added, with lashings of freshly ground black pepper. Served on a bed of plain boiled rice, this was accompanied by oxtail braised in a red wine sauce, roasted carrots and parsnips and baked potatoes. My host told me the entire meal for four cost the equivalent of €4, and it was better than any in an expensive restaurant, (see p 65 and 66 for similar recipes).

In my own home in County Kerry, Sunday dinner was always the same: Roast beef heart, on a bed of onion and carrot accompanied by a sauce made from the juices in the roasting pan and served with mushy peas and colcannon potatoes. This roast heart served nine and there was plenty for everybody. Lamb's hearts are equally tasty and one heart will serve 2-3.

Lambs liver is usually overcooked, even in restaurants. Cooked correctly, it is a delicacy. Toss thin slices in seasoned flour and grill or pan-fry in butter for 3 minutes each side until just pink, not brown. Serve immediately with pan-fried onion and sautéed or creamed potato for a special easy meal.

Venison is now available in supermarkets and is usually the farmed variety. The haunch is excellent roasted and the liver has a special flavour fried as above and served with a simple orange sauce. Venison steaks from farmed animals do not need to be marinated, like the wild, but can benefit from marinating if used on the barbecue.

STEAK & KIDNEY PIE

Serves 4

1 ox kidney
Salted water
240g (8oz) onion,
chopped
480g (8oz) stewing beef
1/4 teasp Herbes de
Provence
1 tbsp chopped parsley
1 teasp butter
1 teasp flour
Pinch black pepper
300ml (1/2pt) brown
stock
Beaten egg to glaze
Puff pastry

✓ Skin and cube ox kidney and stand in salted water for 1 hour to remove strong taste. Pat dry.

✓ Sauté with half the onion until sealed on all sides.

✓ In another pan sauté beef with the remainder of the onions with herbs and parsley. Add butter and flour with black pepper and mix well. Add brown stock and cook for 60 minutes or until tender. Add in the onion and kidney. Pour into pie dish, cool and cover with 240 g (8 oz) puff pastry. Brush with beaten egg and bake at Gas 5; 190C; 375F until brown. To keep pastry from touching meat place a cup upside down in the middle of the meat and rest the pastry on it.

Chicken Legs with
Chutney and Mustard Stuffing

Plum Crumble

LAMBS KIDNEY EPICURIAN

Serves 4 as starter; 2-3 as main course

4-6 lambs kidneys, skinned, halved and diced
1 tbsp oil
1 tbsp onion, finely diced
1 teasp tomato purée
1 teasp flour
1-2 tbsps port
300ml (10fl oz) brown lamb stock (see p 12)
1 teasp french mustard
Black pepper
1 tbsp cream (optional)

▽ Heat oil in heavy saucepan and quickly brown kidneys all over.

▽ Remove from pan.

▽ Add onion and cook slowly for 3 minutes.

▽ Sprinkle on flour and mix well.

▽ Add tomato purée and stock.

▽ Bring to boil and reduce heat for 5 minutes, stirring.

▽ Add mustard and port, and for a smoother finish, add a tablespoon of whipped cream and plenty of freshly ground black pepper.

▽ Return kidneys to sauce and warm gently for 5 minutes.

As a starter serve on a bed of plain boiled rice or as a main course with minted peas and creamed potatoes

SIMPLE OXTAIL CASSEROLE

Serves 4

1 oxtail
1 medium onion, chopped
Oil for frying
1 teasp tomato purée
1 teasp flour
2 glasses red wine or beef stock

✓ Fry oxtail in oil in a heavy saucepan until well sealed and brown. Set aside.

✓ Fry onion over gentle heat for 10-15 minutes until soft.

✓ Add tomato purée and flour and cook for 1 minute.

✓ Add red wine or stock.

✓ Return meat to pot and cover. Cook in a moderate oven Gas 4; 175C; 350F for 2 hours when the tender meat will fall off the bone.

✓ Season with salt and freshly ground black pepper.

Oxtail is a winner. Sometimes butchers give it away as there is so little demand for it. To make the best of it, cook it slowly

BEEF CURRY

**1kg (2.2lb) shin or
shoulder beef, diced
2 tbsps oil
2 onions, chopped
60g (2oz) curry powder
2 cloves garlic
2 tbsps peach chutney
1 cooking apple,
washed, cored & diced
45g (1½oz) flour
2 tbsps tomato purée
1¼lt (2 pints) beef
stock**

✓ In an oven and flame-proof dish heat oil and brown meat quickly all over.

✓ Remove from dish

✓ Add curry powder and flour and cook for 2-3 minutes, stirring

✓ Add onion, garlic & apple, cover and cook slowly for 3-5 minutes

✓ Add tomato purée, chutney and stock and taste for seasoning

✓ Return meat to sauce and cook in oven at Gas 4; 175C; 350F for 1½ hours.

Serve with long-grain rice.

BEEF CASSEROLE WITH RED WINE

Serves 8-9

1kg (2.2lb) shoulder beef in 5cm (2"dice)
60g (2oz) streaky bacon, diced
Oil for browning
2 onions
2-3 cloves garlic, chopped
1 bay leaf, 1 sprig each thyme and rosemary or bouquet garni
Black pepper
2 glasses red wine
15ml (1/2oz) 1 tablesp tomato purée
1 heaped teasp flour
120g (4oz) button mushrooms
120g (4oz) baby onions

✓ Heat oil in a heavy saucepan and brown beef all over to seal in juices.

✓ Remove from pan.

✓ Add onion and allow to sweat (fry gently) for 5 minutes.

✓ Add flour and stir until brown.

✓ Add tomato purée, garlic and wine and bring to boil.

✓ Skim any scum which rises to the top and add herbs and black pepper.

✓ Cook for 1$\frac{1}{2}$ hours in oven at Gas 4; 180C; 350F.

✓ Fry bacon in a frying pan with baby onions and mushrooms. For a slightly sweeter flavour a tablespoon of redcurrant jelly may be added at this stage.

✓ Add into casserole and cook for a further 15-20 minutes.

Serve with matchstick carrots (recipe p 30) and creamed potatoes or rice.

SIRLOIN STEAK PARCELS

1 tbsp groundnut or grapeseed oil

½ teasp english mustard

1 teasp dried basil

120g (4oz) mushrooms, sliced

4 slices cheddar cheese

4 X 300g (10oz) sirloin or striploin steaks

2 large tomatoes, thinly sliced

Salt & black pepper

1 teasp parsley, chopped

Pernod (optional)

✓ Heat oil in a frying pan and seal steaks quickly on all sides

✓ Season with salt & pepper

✓ Place steaks in centre of 4 pieces tin foil and spread with mustard

✓ Top with tomato slices, mushroom, basil and cheese

✓ A teaspoon of Pernod may be added before closing each parcel

✓ Seal foil by pinching edges together and place on a baking sheet

✓ Cook in oven at Gas 5; 190C; 375F for 25 minutes

Serve immediately with a green salad and baked potato

This is a great recipe for a special occasion for hungry individuals who like the richness of meat and strong flavours

HONEY-GLAZED HAM

Serves 4

1.35 kg (3lb) corner or middle gammon joint
Whole cloves
Grated rind and juice 1 orange
45ml (1¹/₂fl oz) 3 tbsps clear honey

✓ Place gammon in a large saucepan and cover with cold water. Bring slowly to the boil then discard water and rinse the joint. This will remove excess salt. Cover with cold water and bring to the boil. Reduce heat and cover the pan and simmer gently for 1 hour.

✓ Drain the gammon. Carefully cut off skin and score the fat in a diamond pattern. Place the meat in a small roasting tin and stud the top with whole cloves.

✓ Mix orange rind and juice with honey and pour over joint, brushing over the sides. Bake at Gas 6; 200C;400F for about 30-40 minutes or until the fat is golden brown. Baste gammon frequently during cooking.
Serve hot or cold. If serving the joint cold, continue to baste with the glaze as it cools.

BARBECUED SPARE RIBS

Serves 8

1.8kg (4lb) pork spare ribs
6 tbsps (90ml) tomato ketchup
3 tbsps (45ml) clear honey
2 tbsps (30ml) red wine vinegar
2 teasp mustard
Pinch Cajun seasoning
Salt and freshly ground black pepper

✓ Pre-heat oven to Gas 7; 220C; 425F.

✓ Cook ribs in a pan of boiling water for 20 minutes and drain.

✓ Line a roasting tin with foil and arrange the spare ribs in a single layer.

✓ Mix together tomato ketchup, honey, wine vinegar, mustard and seasoning and brush over ribs.

✓ Bake for 30 minutes, turning occasionally and basting with any remaining sauce.

Serve on a bed of lettuce with tomato wedges.

PORK CHOPS WITH APPLE & CELERY
STUFFING & REDCURRANT SAUCE

Serves 4

4 chops cut 2.5cm (1") thick

STUFFING:
180g (6oz) breadcrumbs
Salt & pepper
1 teasp Herbes de Provence
30g (2oz) butter
1 stick celery, diced
1 medium sized cooking apple, diced
1 small onion, diced

REDCURRANT SAUCE:
2 tbsps redcurrant jelly added to
1 pint basic brown sauce (see p103)

✓ Melt butter in a pan and add onion, celery, apple, herbs and seasoning. Allow to cool and mix with breadcrumbs

✓ Make a slit in the pork chop near the fat to make a pocket and push stuffing in gently.

✓ Cook in roasting pan in the oven for 25 minutes or until chops are cooked through.

The redcurrant sauce here makes a good contrast with the meat and its flavoursome stuffing

71

STUFFED PORK STEAK
Serves 8

60g (2oz) butter
1/2 cooking apple, peeled, cored and finely diced
2 small leeks, trimmed and sliced
90g (3oz) fresh white breadcrumbs
2 x 360g (12oz) pork steaks
1 medium egg, beaten
1 tbsp each freshly chopped parsley and sage
12 rashers rindless streaky bacon
1 tbsp (15ml) clear honey

To garnish:
Sprig fresh sage
Fried apple wedges and steamed baby carrots

✓ Preheat oven at Gas 4;180C; 350F.

✓ Melt butter in a large frying pan and cook the apple for 2 - 3 mins until turning golden.

✓ Stir in leeks and fry for a further 5 mins until softened.

✓ Remove from heat and stir in fresh breadcrumbs. Cover and leave to cool completely.

✓ Using a sharp knife, cut down the length of each pork steak without cutting right through.

✓ Open out and make two more cuts down the length of the meat so that the meat will become flat and wide.

✓ Stir egg and herbs into stuffing mixture and season with salt and freshly ground black pepper.

✓ Spoon stuffing mixture down the centre of one steak, pressing down well. Place the second steak on top to enclose the stuffing.

✓ Stretch the bacon rashers and wrap around steaks, slightly overlapping each rasher.

✓ Secure with string and wrap in foil and place in oven for 1¹/₂ hours.

✓ Unwrap, brush with honey and roast for a further 30 mins until bacon is golden.

Serve sliced and garnished with sage, apple wedges and carrots.

BLACK AND WHITE PUDDING WITH APPLE SAUCE

Serves 4-6

240g (8oz) black pudding, sliced into 16
240g (8oz) white pudding, sliced into 16
1 tbsp (15ml) grape seed oil for frying
240g (8oz) cooking apples
1 tbsp (15ml) honey
1/₂ tbsps ground cinnamon
Juice 1 large orange

✓ Peel, core and slice apples.

✓ Place in saucepan with cinnamon, honey and orange juice. Cook until tender.

✓ Whiz in liquidiser or mash thoroughly. Allow to cool.

✓ When diners are seated, heat oil in frying pan and cook pudding on both sides for 3 to 4 minutes until crisp.

✓ Drain on kitchen paper.

✓ Swirl some apple sauce onto four individual plates and sit slices of pudding on top. Serve immediately.

The flavour of the puddings contrasts perfectly with the tart apple, subtly flavoured with orange and cinnamon. This makes a superb starter or lunch dish. It can become a main course by serving with creamy mashed potato, new potatoes, or a layered bacon and potato cake (see p.25).

MUSTARD GLAZED LAMB CUTLETS

2 cutlets per person, well trimmed
2 tbsps Dijon mustard
3 tbsps brown sugar

✓ With a pastry brush, coat cutlets with mustard and then in brown sugar.

✓ Cook on barbecue or under grill for 4 minutes a side and serve with baked potatoes and salad.

BAKED POTATOES

✓ Wash a large potato per person. Prick with a fork and bake in the oven for 50 minutes at Gas 4; 180C; 350F. Finish off on side of the barbecue for 10-15 minutes.

73

RAGOUT OF LAMB IN IRISH MIST

Serves 4

1kg (2lb) trimmed and diced shoulder of lamb
250ml (8fl oz) red wine
1pt (500ml) brown lamb bone stock
(see p 12)
120g (4oz) diced onion
1 bayleaf
1 teasp Herbes de Provence
1 tbsp (15ml) olive oil
2 cloves garlic
1 level tbsps wholemeal flour
1 level tbsps tomato purée
1 teasp redcurrant jelly
1 liqueur glass Irish Mist
1 teasp redcurrant jelly

✓ Place lamb into a bowl, add bay leaf, herbs, half of diced onion and wine.

✓ Cover and stand for at least 6 hours.

✓ Remove meat from marinade and reserve.

✓ Heat oil in a heavy based saucepan and fry onion and garlic.

✓ Add lamb and fry briskly.

✓ Add flour and cook for a few minutes.

✓ Add tomato purée, stir well.

✓ Pour on marinade and stock and bring to the boil.

✓ Transfer to an ovenproof lidded casserole and cook at Gas 5; 190C; 375F for 90 minutes or until meat is tender.

✓ 10 minutes before serving remove from oven and add Irish Mist and blackcurrant jelly.

✓ Allow to stand in the saucepan with lid on for 10 minutes to allow flavours to blend.

Serve with potatoes and boiled carrots.

This is a heartwarming flavoursome dish, even without the Irish Mist

3 Days of
NO-NONSENSE
Festive
Dining

In times past, roast turkey, associated with Christmas in Ireland since time immemorial, made just one annual appearance on the domestic menu cycle, on Christmas Day.

Today however, turkey manifests itself on our hotel and restaurant menus nationwide at least once a week. Over exposure to this particular product brings a heavy burden to bear on the home cook to present traditional Christmas dinner in an alternative palate-pleasing way.

It is beyond doubt that larger birds will have more mature flavour than smaller turkeys, so I recommend a 14/15lb hen turkey even for the smaller family.

If you would like to save yourself some money, and at the same time serve your family and friends delicious food over the Christmas break, then this three day menu cycle is for you. But first you must make a series of menus and do your shopping based on requirements dictated by such dishes. Go shopping without a list spells disaster!

Order your turkey in plenty of time,and ask your butcher to: (a) remove legs and bone them; (b) to remove both breasts. When you collect them, please make sure you also have the carcass and the leg bones, and the giblets for stock.

CHRISTMAS MENU (DAY 1)

Melon Crown with Fresh Fruit and Puréed Strawberry

🎁

Spicy Parsnip and Apple Soup

🎁

Roast Stuffed Breasts and Leg of Turkey
Maple-glazed Ham on the Bone
Pan-fried Sprouts
Roast Potatoes
Creamed Potatoes
Fresh Gravy
Cranberry Sauce

🎁

Christmas Trifle

If having a bottle of red wine with your Christmas dinner, stand it in your kitchen overnight, and then open two hours before serving. This will help to make the 'plonkiest' of wines palatable.

CHRISTMAS MENU (DAY 2)

Turkey and Ham Chowder

🎁

Turkey Breast fried in Breadcrumbs with Bacon Rolls,
Pan-fried Pineapple and Banana
Red Cabbage
Creamed Potato

CHRISTMAS MENU (DAY 3)

Roast Stuffed Turkey Leg

🎁

Turkey and Ham Flan

77

MELON CROWN WITH FRESH FRUIT AND PURÉED STRAWBERRY

Allow **one small melon** for two persons.

✓ On Christmas morning put a piece of string or rubber band around the centre of the fruit.

✓ With a small sharp knife cut through the flesh in a zigzag manner, all around the string or band. When complete, pull apart for two lovely 'crowns' of melon.

✓ Take a narrow slice from the end of each half to secure standing.

✓ In a separate bowl, combine **60g (2oz) black and green grapes, one kiwi, 60g (2oz) fresh strawberries, one banana, two plums and one red apple,** washed, cored but not peeled.

✓ Roughly chop all ingredients, pour over **1 pint of 7up** over fruit to keep it from discolouring. Cool in refrigerator.

✓ Open a **1lb tin of strawberries**, discard half of its juices and liquidise fruit and remaining liquid together.

✓ Chill serving plates in the fridge for 1 hour.

✓ When ready to serve, cover the base of the plate with puréed strawberry, stand one melon crown in the centre of each plate (make sure seeds are removed).

✓ Strain off liquid from fresh fruit and fill the centre of the melon crown.

✓ Garnish with lime and serve.

SPICY PARSNIP AND APPLE SOUP

Serves 6

30g (1oz) butter
1 onion, chopped
1 clove garlic, crushed
1 medium potato
1 parsnip
1 eating apple
1 tbsp white flour
1 teasp curry powder
2 litres (3¹/₄ pints) turkey stock
Salt and pepper
Low-fat natural yogurt and chopped parsley to serve.

✓ Peel and chop potatoes, parsnip and apple.

✓ Cook in butter with onion on a low heat for 10 minutes.

✓ Add the flour and curry powder and cook for a couple of minutes.

✓ Add the stock, stir well, bring to the boil and simmer for 30 minutes.

✓ When cooked, blend until smooth, adding more stock if the mixture is too thick.

✓ Season and serve garnished with a swirl of natural yogurt and a sprinkling of parsley.

Make the day before for extra flavour

STUFFING FOR LEG & BREAST OF TURKEY

240g (8oz) white breadcrumbs
Salt and pepper to taste
1 tbsp freshly chopped parsley
1 heaped teasp Herbes de Provence
60g (2oz) butter
60g (2oz) diced onion
2 sticks celery, diced
1 medium cooking apple, washed and grated.

✓ Put breadcrumbs, parsley, pepper and salt into a bowl.

✓ Melt butter in a frying pan or flame proof casserole, add onion, celery, apple and herbs

✓ Sweat for 4 minutes over a very gentle heat. Allow to cool.

✓ Mix all ingredients together.

Stuffing is now ready to use.

ROAST STUFFED TURKEY BREAST

☑ Refrigerate one turkey breast for use on Day 2
☑ Make a pocket in one side of the other turkey breast, dust with freshly ground black pepper and if liked some grated lemon rind.
☑ Fill pocket with stuffing.
☑ Grease a sheet of tin foil with grape seed oil and wrap around turkey breast - this is now ready for the oven.

ROASTED AND STUFFED TURKEY LEGS

☑ Flatten out the turkey legs and remove the sinews by sliding knife along the sinews while pulling on them, keeping the flesh as intact as possible. To flatten, put between two sheets of wet greaseproof paper, and pound with a rolling pin. Discard greaseproof and sprinkle with freshly ground black pepper and stuffing.
☑ Roll up and wrap in greased tin foil like a Christmas cracker.
☑ Refrigerate one turkey leg to keep for Day 3.
☑ Heat the oven to Gas 4; 180C; 350F and put breast and leg in to cook at least two hours before dinner service is planned.
☑ Fifteen minutes before time, roll back foil from breast to allow to brown slightly. Stand out of heat for ten minutes before carving.

Before placing the stuffing on the meat try a light coating of prepared cranberry sauce spread on the meat, it provides a beautiful after taste.

An alternative stuffing for the turkey legs would be 90g (3oz) white pudding, removed from its wrapping and mashed with a fork. Spread over the turkey leg meat, and roll in the usual way.

80

TURKEY GRAVY

Do not contaminate the beautiful flavours of turkey and stuffing with the use of convenience gravies.

If you are roasting a few chickens before Christmas, put the liquids of the roasting tin in a container and keep refrigerated until needed. Turn upside down, and remove the 'slab' of gelatine from the underneath. Put this with one pint of turkey stock into a small pot, boil and strain. Now whisk in one tablespoon of tomato purée and thicken with a little cornflour mixed with cold stock. Re-boil and you have a magical gravy, (all of this can be done the night before).

SPROUTS

✓ Discard outer leaves and place in salted cold water.
✓ Bring to the boil for eight minutes.
✓ Strain off in a colander and allow the cold tap to gently run over the sprouts for 2-3 minutes until they are quite cold.
✓ Leave aside until needed.
✓ 7 minutes before serving, add one tablespoon of butter to a heavy based pot, melt and add sprouts.
✓ Grated nutmeg and freshly ground black pepper are a lovely addition. Cook over a low heat for five minutes, shaking pot often.

ROAST POTATOES

These should be cooked in a separate tin from the turkey.
✓ Bring peeled potatoes to the boil for five minutes, rinse with cold water and dry well in kitchen paper.
✓ Toss in hot fat or oil, making sure each potato is coated in the oil. Roast for just one hour.

CHRISTMAS TRIFLE

Serves 4-6

Three days in advance, make your own sponge using 6 eggs, 180g (6oz) plain flour and 180g (6oz) sugar, in the normal way.

480g (1lb) tin strawberries
480g (1lb) tin of peaches
Juice two large oranges
Large whiskey measure of Irish Cream Liqueur
600ml (20fl oz) custard

◁ Cut sponge in thin slices, liquidise peaches and strawberries separately, pour into separate jugs, squeeze oranges and now you are ready to combine ingredients.

◁ To combine this trifle, use a glass bowl and on the base put a layer of sponge, now a layer of puréed peaches, then a layer of sponge and a layer of strawberries.

◁ Continue in this way until all the sponge is in the bowl, and pour over all remaining puréed fruits as well as the fresh orange juice.

◁ Spoon over Irish Cream Liqueur and allow to stand in a cold room for two hours.

◁ Cover with one pint of custard and finally, just before service, pipe on some freshly whipped cream. Decorate with cherries and serve.

This trifle does not have a long shelf-life, and should be made not more than six hours before consumption.

TURKEY BREAST FRIED IN BREADCRUMBS

✓ Cut breast remaining from Day 1 into 2.5cm (1") steaks.

✓ Coat with seasoned flour, eggwash (1 egg mixed with 300ml (10fl oz) milk) and coat well with breadcrumbs, pressing well into meat.

✓ Leave to stand for thirty minutes before cooking.

✓ When ready to cook, put a little grape seed oil in a frying pan, and brown steaks on all sides.

✓ Finish off in a moderate oven for twenty minutes.

Serve with bacon rolls, pan-fried pineapple and banana, red cabbage and creamed potato.

TURKEY AND HAM CHOWDER

Serves 10

30g (1oz) butter
1 tbsp flour
60g (2oz) onion, diced
120g (4oz) parsnip, diced
120g (4oz) carrot, diced
3 sticks celery, diced
2 large potatoes, peeled and diced
1 tbsp parsley, chopped
Salt & freshly ground black pepper
1 tbsp flour
2¹/₂ litres (4 pints) turkey stock (see page 103)

✓ In a large heavy-based pot, melt butter, add all vegetables, cover and sweat with the lid on for 5 minutes over low heat. Please be careful - do not allow to brown.

✓ Add chopped parsley, some freshly ground black pepper, salt and flour. Mix and allow to stand for 1 minute.

✓ Bring turkey stock to the boil and pour over vegetables.

✓ Bring to the boil, reduce heat and cook slowly for 10 minutes.

✓ Dice any leftover turkey and ham pieces and add to soup.

✓ Finish with a little pouring cream

Serve with garlic bread to your friends around the Christmas fire. They will love you forever.

TURKEY AND HAM FLAN Serves 4-6

180g (6oz) cream flour
120g (4oz) cold butter
1 egg
1 egg yolk
125ml (4fl oz) milk
125ml (4fl oz) pouring cream
90g (3oz) cooked ham, diced
90g (3oz) cooked turkey, diced
1 teasp onion, diced finely

Pastry can be made some days in advance:
✓ Sieve flour into a bowl and add butter, and with your fingers, rub to make texture of breadcrumbs, then gather into a ball.

✓ Wrap in greaseproof and keep in the 'fridge until needed.

✓ Bring to kitchen temperature for one hour before rolling out and lining a 9" quiche tin. It is not necessary to bake the pastry blind.

✓ Sprinkle ham, turkey and onion on pastry case, pour over egg, milk and cream mixed together and bake in the centre of the over at Gas 4; 180C; 328F for about 30 minutes.

✓ Turn out and serve hot from the oven with a green salad and baked potato.

MAPLE-GLAZED HAM ON THE BONE

Few of us have pans large enough to cook a ham, so cook it in the oven, wrapped in a tent of tin foil. This method also works well for cooking a smaller ham joint.

✓ Soak a full ham joint overnight in a large container of cold water, to remove any excess salt.

✓ Crisscross two long sheets of double-width foil in a large roasting tin and place the ham on top. Add 600ml (1pt) cider, a quartered onion, juice 1 orange and a few fresh bay leaves. Make a loose tent with the foil around the ham, then cook at Gas 3; 160°C; 325°F for 4 hours (or twenty minutes per lb. if cooking a smaller joint).

✓ 40 minutes before the end of the cooking time, remove the ham from the oven (reserve the juices) and carefully cut away the rind to leave a thin, even coating of fat. Score the fat into diamonds then stud with cloves.

✓ Mix 3 tablespoons maple syrup with rind 1 orange and 2 tablespoons ready-made English mustard. Brush the mixture over the outside of the ham then return to the oven at Gas 6; 200°C; 400°F for 40 minutes until it turns golden.

TIRAMISU

24 sponge fingers (lady-fingers)
5 tbsps instant coffee powder
300ml (1/2pt) hot water
3 tbsps rum
300ml (1/2pt) double cream
250g (8oz) Mascarpone cheese
60g (2oz) icing sugar
2 tbsps cocoa powder

✓ Cover the bottom of a serving dish with half the sponge fingers.

✓ Combine the instant coffee powder and hot water and soak the sponge fingers in half of the coffee and half of the rum for a few minutes

✓ Whip the cream, stir in the Mascarpone and sift in the icing sugar.

✓ Spoon half the Mascarpone mixture in a layer over the sponge fingers

✓ Sift half of the cocoa powder over the Mascarpone mixture. Make another layer of sponge fingers in the same way, using the remaining coffee and rum, Mascarpone and cocoa powder.

Chill the tiramisu for at least 4 hours before serving
This is a light alternative to Christmas pudding and can be made a day ahead.

ALMOND ICING (MARZIPAN)

720g (1 1/2lb) ground almonds
480g (1lb) icing sugar
240g (1/2lb) caster sugar
4 eggs
Juice 1 lemon
1 teasp vanilla essence
1 dessertsp each rum and orangeflower water

✓ Crush icing sugar with rolling pin and sieve well.

✓ Mix the dry ingredients.

✓ Beat eggs and gradually add flavourings.

✓ Mix to a paste, first with a wooden spoon and then with the hand.

✓ Having kneaded the paste, wrap in greaseproof paper, put in a covered jar or tin and leave until next day when it will be easier to handle. See instructions page 86.

A word of warning: while it is essential to work the marzipan into a smooth paste, it must not be overhandled, otherwise it will become crumbly and brittle.

85

TO APPLY ALMOND ICING
TO CHRISTMAS CAKE

Christmas cakes need a little special preparation before putting on the almond icing.

✓ For best results, you need an even surface. If the cake has not risen evenly, you may: (a) turn the cake upside down, or (b) camouflage any unevenness with almond paste. If, in spite of the precautions taken against burning, the bottom or sides have burnt spots, grate off the burnt parts with a fine bread-grater or a serrated knife.

✓ Brush off any loose crumbs, and then give the cake a coat of slightly-beaten egg white.

✓ Knead the icing a little, divide it in two, and on a pastry board sprinkled with caster sugar, roll out one piece into a round large enough to cover the top of the cake.

✓ Put the round of icing on the cake, and then run the rolling pin lightly over it to make it even.

✓ Take a piece of string and measure the circumference of the cake.

✓ Roll out the icing for the sides in two even pieces, this will be easier to manage than one long strip.

✓ Press the two lengths of icing into position and make the sides smooth and symmetrical by rolling a jam-jar or milk bottle around the sides.

✓ The cake may now be covered and put away in a dry place for a week when it will be ready for royal icing.

Good
Old-Fashioned
Cakes and Puddings

It is rewarding and psychologically uplifting to experience the 'born again' re-emergence of some of the traditional classical puddings of our childhood.

Someone once wrote "a hot steamy pudding presented on a cold winter's day is the gastronomic equivalent of a hug from a loved one". What a wonderful description!

In everyday domestic cookery, I feel a 3 course main meal may be too much, so every other day serve a starter or a dessert with the main course.

HOT FRESH FRUIT SALAD

Serves 5-6

✓ Combine **480g (16oz)** of whatever **fresh fruit** you can lay your hands on, remembering the attractiveness of diversity of colour.

✓ If fruits are prepared ahead of time then you must use a 'holding liquid' to keep fruits from going brown or oxidising: bring to the boil **3 cups water 60g (2oz) sugar, 1 slice lemon, 1 bay leaf, a few whole cloves and 3 or 4 black peppercorns.** When boiling point is reached, allow to stand to infuse, and when perfectly cool, pour over chopped fruit.

✓ When ready to serve, heat a heavy-based frying pan, and sprinkle with castor sugar.

✓ When the sugar goes brown strain fruit and add to frying pan.

✓ Return to the heat for 1 minute, stirring all the time.

✓ Add the juice of ½ **orange** and finally heat a whiskey measure full of **Tia Maria or Cointreau** in your soup ladle. Ignite and pour over fruit in frying pan. This looks rather spectacular if done in the presence of your guests, don't worry about the flame; beyond taking reasonable care, there is no danger involved as the flames will die down once the alcohol has burned off.

Serve immediately.

This is ideal in winter when cold fruit is unappetising.

BREAD AND BUTTER PUDDING

10 slices white bread,
crusts removed
90g (3oz) sultanas
4 tbsps apricot jam,
sieved
4 eggs
180g (6oz) caster sugar
600ml (1pt) milk
300ml ($1/_4$pt) double
cream
1 teasp vanilla essence
120g (4oz) unsalted
butter

☑ Grease an ovenproof dish.

☑ Sandwich buttered bread with sultanas in middle and spread jam on outside. Line the dish with the slices.

☑ Beat the eggs and caster sugar in a bowl until a smooth foaming mixture is reached.

☑ Bring cream and milk to the boil, add vanilla essence and pour over eggs, whisking all the time.

☑ Ladle this over the bread and leave to soak for 15 minutes.

☑ Bake for 45 minutes approx. in a large baking dish, with water half way up the sides, at Gas 5; 190C; 375F until golden brown on top and firm to the touch.

This is so easy to make and so good to eat. It is one of my all-time favourite hot desserts.

PLUM CRUMBLE

Serves 5

90g (3oz) butter
180g (5oz) plain flour
60g (2oz) sugar
30g (1oz) porridge oats
60g (2oz) hazelnuts, chopped and toasted
960g (2lb) plums, halved and stoned
30-60ml (1-2fl oz) 2-4 tbsps honey
Rind 1 orange

✓ Pre-heat oven to Gas 6; 200C; 400F.

✓ Rub butter into flour until mixture resembles fine breadcrumbs.

✓ Stir in sugar, porridge oats and hazelnuts.

✓ Place plums in a pan with water, honey and orange rind.

✓ Bring to boil and simmer for 15 minutes, uncovered.

✓ Transfer to an ovenproof dish and top with crumble mixture.

✓ Bake for 35-40 minutes until golden.

BLACKBERRY AND APPLE CRUMBLE

Serves 5

FILLING:
6 large cooking apples
90g (3oz) butter
180g (6oz) blackberries (fresh or frozen)
60g (2oz) caster sugar

CRUMBLE TOPPING:
6 tbsps flour
3 tbsps butter
6 tbsps heavy brown sugar
6 tbsps finely ground blanched almonds

✓ Pre-heat oven to Gas 5; 190C; 375F.

✓ Place apples in a pan with butter. Sauté over medium heat until tender (about 10 minutes). Allow to cool.

✓ Transfer to a greased ovenproof dish and top with blackcurrants and sugar.

✓ Rub butter into flour until mixture resembles fine breadcrumbs.

✓ Stir in sugar and almonds. Allow to stand for 15 minutes before sprinkling on fruit mixture.

Bake for 35-40 minutes until golden.
Serve with a scoop of vanilla ice-cream.

RHUBARB MERINGUE SLICE

Serves 4-6

275g (9oz) pastry
150g (5oz) cream flour
60g (2oz) ground
almonds
30g (1oz) caster sugar
8 sticks rhubarb
Juice large orange
3 tbsps water
75g (3½oz) butter
2 tbsps sugar

Meringue Topping:
3 large egg whites
Pinch salt
200g (7oz) caster sugar

✓ Mix together the flour, ground almonds and caster sugar.

✓ Cut the butter into pieces and allow to come to room temperature. Rub into flour mixture until it resembles fine breadcrumbs.

✓ Add enough water to make a workable dough, using a fork.

✓ Knead lightly on a floured surface and allow to rest for 30 minutes in the fridge.

✓ Roll out into two 10cm by 30cm strips. Place on a floured non-stick baking sheet and cook at 180C (gas 5) for 20 minutes. Cool completely.

✓ Top and tail rhubarb into 9cm pieces, and place in rows in a roasting tin. Add the orange juice and sugar, cover with tinfoil and bake for 20 minutes at 180C (gas 5). Remove from oven and cool completely.

✓ Whisk the egg whites with a pinch of salt, until they form soft peaks. Add the caster sugar and beat for 3 more minutes.

✓ Remove the cooled rhubarb from the roasting tin and place on top of pastry sheets.

✓ Put meringue into a piping bag and cover the rhubarb. Place into the hot oven for 3-4 minutes until the meringue is golden brown.

✓ Strain the juices from the cooking of the rhubarb and use to drizzle around the portions of rhubarb slices on the service plate.

HONEY & SESAME BAKLAVA

Serves 8

PASTRY:
180g (6oz)chopped almonds
45ml (1¹/₂fl oz) 3 tbsps sesame seeds
240g (8oz) walnut pieces
5ml (1 teasp) ground cinnamon
Large pinch ground cloves
240g (8oz) filo pastry
60-90g (2-3oz) butter, melted
8 whole cloves

✓ Pre-heat oven to Gas 4; 180C; 350F.

✓ In a bowl mix together the almonds, sesame seeds, walnuts, cinnamon and cloves.

✓ Brush a 23-25.5cm (9-10")shallow round ovenproof dish with melted butter.

✓ Brush 4 sheets of filo with melted butter and layer in the dish.

✓ Spoon half the walnut mixture into the dish on top of the filo.

✓ Repeat, finishing with a layer of filo then tuck the ends of the filo down the sides of the dish.

✓ Score into 8 portions with a sharp knife and press a whole clove into the centre of each portion.

✓ Bake for 45 minutes.

✓ When the pastry is brown enough (after about 30 minutes), cover loosely with foil to prevent it from burning.

SYRUP:
120g (4oz) granulated sugar
60ml (2fl oz) clear honey
30ml (1fl oz) lemon juice
15ml (¹/₂fl oz) 1 tablesp vanilla essence
90ml (3fl oz) water

✓ Dissolve sugar and honey in water over gentle heat.

✓ Increase heat and allow to bubble for 5 minutes

✓ Remove from heat and stir in lemon juice and vanilla.

✓ When the Baklava comes out of the oven, carefully spoon the warm syrup over it.

Allow to cool before serving.

HONEY MULLED FRUIT BRULÉE

Serves 6

240g (8oz) dried fruits - apricots, apples, pears, peaches
500ml (16fl oz) water
Pared rind 1 lemon
2 cloves
1 cinnamon stick
2fl oz (60ml) clear honey
200g creme fraiche
300ml (1/2pt) greek yoghurt
90g (3oz) soft brown sugar
Few flaked almonds (optional)

✓ Place fruits in a bowl and pour over water.

✓ Leave to stand, covered, overnight. Transfer to a pan and add lemon rind, cloves, cinnamon and honey.

✓ Add enough water to cover fruits.

✓ Heat slowly to boiling point then lower heat to simmer, covered, for 15-20 minutes.

✓ Drain, reserving 150ml (1/4pt) liquid. Allow fruit to cool slightly before transferring to a heatproof dish. Remove lemon rind and spices from reserved liquid and pour over fruit.

✓ Mix together creme fraiche and yoghurt and top with sugar and flaked almonds, if using.

✓ Chill for 30 minutes, then place under a pre-heated grill until bubbling. Serve immediately.

FRIED BANANAS

Serves 4

Juice ½ lemon
4 bananas, cut in half lengthwise
60g (2oz) butter
30g (1oz) flaked almonds
30ml (2 tbsps) clear honey

✓ Sprinkle lemon juice over bananas.

✓ Melt the butter in a frying pan, add bananas and cook, turning once, until browned on both sides.

✓ Transfer to a warmed serving plate.

✓ Add almonds to butter remaining in the pan and cook until lightly browned.

✓ Stir in honey and heat through. Pour over the bananas and serve immediately.

BANOFFI PIE

Serves 6 - 8

400g (14oz) can condensed milk
250g (8oz) plain (all purpose) flour
125g (4oz) unsalted butter
8 tbsps cold water
3 bananas
300ml (½pt) double cream
1 teasp instant coffee powder
1 teasp hot water

✓ Leave the can of milk unopened and place in a saucepan of water, so that it is submerged. Bring the water to the boil and boil the can for 4 hours

✓ Sift the flour into a bowl and rub in the butter until the mixture resembles breadcrumbs. Mix in the water and bring the mixture together lightly with your fingertips. Wrap in clingfilm or greaseproof paper and chill for at least 30 minutes.

✓ Line a 25cm (10 inch) flan tin with baking parchment. Roll out the pastry into a 25cm (10 inch) circle and line the flan tin with it.

✓ Bake the pastry base in a preheated oven at 190C 375F Gas Mark 5 for 15 minutes. Leave to cool in the tin.

✓ Open the boiled can of condensed milk – if it is still hot, open it under a tea towel. The milk will have turned to a toffee-like consistency. Spread a single layer of the "toffee" over the cooked pastry base. Slice the bananas and spread out over the toffee layer.

✓ Whip the cream until softly stiff. Dissolve the instant coffee powder in the hot water and fold into the cream. Spoon or pipe the cream over the bananas. Chill until ready to serve.

94

PEARS IN RED WINE

Serves 4

4 pears, not over-ripe
2 glasses good quality
red table wine.
1 pint water
90g (3oz) loaf or cubed
sugar
1 slice lemon
1 cinnamon stick
1 tbsp arrowroot

✓ In a saucepan just big enough to take pears base side down, add water and sugar.
✓ Bring to the boil and add wine.
✓ Return to the boil, add lemon and cinnamon stick.
✓ Peel pears and cook in liquid for approximately 30 minutes or until pears are soft.
✓ When cooked, transfer pears to serving glass.
✓ Mix arrowroot with a little water, and pour on to boiling juices.
✓ Remove cinnamon stick and lemon.
✓ When liquid clears and thickens, pour over pears - allow to cool for 4 hours before serving.

STRAWBERRY MOUSSE

240g (8oz) fresh
strawberries
60g (2oz) sugar
175ml (6fl oz) water
1 sachet (15g) gelatine
10fl oz (1/2pt) cream
4 egg whites

Fresh strawberries
simply eaten with caster
sugar and cream are
magnificent. When they
are plentiful and cheap,
this dessert makes a
welcome change

✓ Wash fruit and remove stalks and purée in a liquidiser or mash well.
✓ Bring water and sugar to the boil in a heavy saucepan.
✓ Remove from heat and sprinkle over gelatine to melt.
✓ Whip the cream lightly.
✓ Add the strawberry puree to the gelatine mixture and mix well.
✓ Fold in the cream and refrigerate until about to set.
✓ Beat egg whites until they stand in peaks, gently fold into the fruit and cream.
✓ Place in refrigerator to set or divide into individual moulds. (Serves 4-6)

MERINGUE ROULADE WITH PEACHES

Serves 4-6

4 egg whites
225g (7oz) caster sugar
300ml (10fl oz) whipped cream
2 peaches, sliced very thinly
Peach slices to decorate

✓ Pre-heat the oven to Gas 4; 180C; 350F.

✓ Line a Swiss roll tin with foil and oil it slightly.

✓ Place egg whites into a spotlessly clean bowl of a food mixer.

✓ Break up with the whisk for 30 seconds then add all the castor sugar together.

✓ Whisk at full speed until it holds a stiff peak (4-5 minutes approx.)

✓ Spread the meringue gently over the lined Swiss roll tin.

✓ Bake for 20 minutes or until it begins to colour but is soft in the centre.

✓ Turn out on to grease proof paper sprinkled with caster sugar and allow to cool for 20 minutes.

✓ Spread with some cream and peach slices.

✓ Roll meringue lengthways in Swiss roll fashion and slide onto an oblong serving plate.

✓ To decorate, alternate rosettes of piped cream with slices of peach.

CARRAGEEN MOSS MOULD ON BED OF PURÉED RHUBARB

I always look forward to spring and the arrival of rhubarb on the market. It has so many uses and makes a delicious crumble. But have you ever tasted Carrageen moss mould on a bed of puréed rhubarb? Quite delicious and so good for you.

Carrageen moss is an edible algae found around our shores but particularly on the Aran Islands, where natives pick it from the sea shore at low tide, and save it lovingly before selling to tourists and natives alike. You will find Carrageen at the health counter in most good stores. To make 5 glorious portions of this health-giving dessert, soak $1/_2$ oz dried carrageen in tepid water for 5 minutes.

CARRAGEEN MOSS MOULD

✓ Put 1 litre milk with some lemon rind in a heavy-based saucepan.
✓ Add carrageen and slowly bring to the boil, stirring all the time for approximately 12 to 15 minutes until thickened.
✓ Add 60g (2oz) sugar or 3 tablespoons honey and 1 whiskey measure Irish cream liqueur, before straining through a fine sieve.
✓ Allow to stand until cool and chill in refrigerator for 3 to 4 hours.

RHUBARB PURÉE

✓ Wash and chop 6 rhubarb stalks and place in a saucepan.
✓ Add $1/_2$ cup cold tea, bring to the boil and simmer for 10 minutes. Sweeten to taste.
✓ Refrigerate until cold.

To serve, pour rhubarb purée on to individual plates and place a wedge of carrageen mould in the centre.

CREME CARAMELS

Serves 4

SYRUP:
120g (4oz) caster sugar
60ml (4 tbsps) water

CUSTARD:
600ml (1pt) milk
4 medium eggs
2.5ml (1/₂teasp) vanilla essence
60g (2oz) caster sugar

✓ Place caster sugar in a pan with water and heat gently until dissolved.

✓ Increase the heat and boil the syrup rapidly, without stirring, until the mixture turns a deep golden caramel.

✓ Remove from the heat and pour into the bases of 4 150 ml (1/₄pt) ovenproof moulds. Leave to cool.

✓ Pour 600ml/1pt milk into a pan and heat until almost boiling, then remove from the heat.

✓ In a bowl, whisk together: eggs, vanilla essence and caster sugar.

✓ Whisk the hot milk into the eggs, then strain the milk mixture into the moulds. Cover with lightly greased foil and place in a shallow roasting tin.

✓ Pour enough hot water into the roasting tin to come halfway up the sides of the moulds. Bake in a preheated oven at Gas 3; 160C; 325F for 45 mins to 1 hr until just set.

✓ Remove moulds from the tin and leave to cool, then chill in the fridge overnight.

To serve, gently loosen the edges of each crème caramel and turn out on to small plates.

SUMMER PUDDING

6-8 large slices white and brown bread with crusts removed
120-180g (4-6oz) granulated sugar
6 tbsps water
240g (8oz) small strawberries
240g (8oz) raspberries
240g (8oz) blackcurrants
240g (8oz) redcurrants

✓ Put one slice bread to one side for the top. Use the remainder to line the base and sides of a pudding bowl.

✓ Place redcurrants and blackcurrants in a saucepan and add the sugar and water. Bring to the boil and simmer until barely tender, stirring all the time.

✓ Add the strawberries and raspberries and cook for one further minute.

✓ Turn the mixture carefully into the bread-lined bowl. Place the extra slice of bread on top and bend over the tops of the bread from the sides towards the centre.

✓ Place a saucer on top, pressing down a little until the juice rises to the top.

✓ Leave overnight to set. Turn out onto a plate and serve with natural yoghurt or low fat fromage frais.

A delicious,easy to make pudding. Quantities and fruits given may be varied. Adjust sugar to sweetness of fruits.

HONEY TEA BREAD

Makes 1 900g (2lb loaf)

240g (8oz) raisins
90g (3oz) set honey
300ml (¹/₂pt) freshly made strong tea
2 eggs, size 3, lightly beaten
300g (10oz) whole-wheat flour
2.5ml (¹/₂teasp) ground mixed spice
15ml (1 tbsp) baking powder

▽ Preheat oven to Gas 4; 180C; 350F.

▽ Place raisins in a bowl.

▽ Stir honey into tea and pour this over the raisins.

▽ Allow to soak for 2 hours.

▽ Stir the eggs into the raisin mixture

▽ Mix the flour with the spice and baking powder and add to the raisin mixture.

▽ Transfer to a greased 900 g (2 lb) tin and bake for about 1 hour 10 minutes.

▽ Cool on a wire rack and serve sliced and buttered.

CHOCOLATE REFRIGERATOR CAKE

120g (4oz) plain chocolate
120g (4oz) butter
1 egg
30g (1oz) sugar
1 teasp instant coffee powder
Vanilla essence
120g (4oz) cold mashed potato
120g (4oz) cake or biscuit crumbs
120g (4oz) marzipan

- ◁ Line a small loaf tin with greased paper.
- ◁ Melt chocolate in a basin over a pan of hot water or microwave on high for 1 minute.
- ◁ Melt butter separately.
- ◁ Beat egg and sugar together with coffee powder and vanilla essence.
- ◁ Beat in butter, then chocolate and finally fold in potato and crumbs.
- ◁ Press into the tin and chill in the fridge for at least 2 hours.
- ◁ Turn out on to a board.
- ◁ Roll out the marzipan and use to cover the top and sides of the cake.
- ◁ Pinch the edges together.
- ◁ Return to the fridge for a further $1/2$ hour before serving.

SHORTCRUST PASTRY

250g (8oz) flour
1 teasp salt
2 teasp caster sugar
(optional)
75g (2¹/₂oz) butter
75g (2¹/₂oz) lard
60ml (2fl oz) cold water

1 egg yolk (optional)

✓ Sieve the flour, salt and sugar together into a bowl.

✓ Add butter and lard, cut into cubes and rub gently with the fingertips to make a mixture like fine breadcrumbs.

✓ Add egg yolk mixed with water (the egg yolk makes a slightly heavier pastry) or just water to make a paste. Do not work the pastry any more than necessary to get it into a ball.

✓ Wrap in clingfilm and refrigerate until required, then roll out lightly.

The sugar may be omitted for a savoury pastry.

BROWN BREAD

Yields 2 x 1lb loaves

3 cups brown flour
1 cup plain white flour
700 ml (1¹/₄ pints)
buttermilk
Pinch salt
1 tbsp porridge oatlets
1 tbsp bran
1 teasp bread soda
30g (1oz) butter, melted
1 tbsp dark brown
sugar
1 tbsp wheatgerm

✓ Sieve white flour and add in remaining dry ingredients.

✓ Add buttermilk and butter and mix lightly.

✓ Place in a greased tin and bake in a pre-heated oven for 50-60 minutes Gas 6; 200C; 400F.

Cool on a wire rack.

FRANK'S BASICS

ROUX

✓ In a heavy based saucepan melt 15g (1oz) butter over gentle heat.

✓ Off the heat add the same amount of flour as butter, mix with a wooden spoon and, back on the heat cook out the roux slowly stirring all the time with a wooden spoon.

✓ After 3 mins. allow to cool.

BROWN SAUCE

✓ Add 300ml (10fl oz) well reduced brown stock (p12) to the roux and cook for 3 minutes.

✓ Add 1 teaspoon of tomato purée for a richer sauce.

CHEESE SAUCE

✓ Add 300ml (10fl oz) milk to the roux and cook for 3 minutes.

✓ Add 1 teaspoon French mustard for a sauce with a bit of zing.

FISH STOCK

✓ In a large saucepan melt a knob of butter and cook 1 onion, finely chopped, until soft but not brown.

✓ Add 750g (1¼lb) fish bones, 250ml (8fl oz) white wine or juice of ½ lemon, 1 litre (1¾pt) water and 2 teaspoons black peppercorns and a bunch of herbs.

✓ Bring to the boil and skim off any scum which rises to the top.

✓ Simmer, uncovered, for 30 minutes and strain before using.

TURKEY STOCK MADE FROM RAW BONES

✓ Place the turkey bones in a roasting dish and put into a moderately hot oven Gas 4;180C; 350F and roast for at least 1 hour.

✓ Remove into a large pot or saucepan, with cold water well covering the bones

✓ Add ½ teaspoon of salt, a 2.5kg (3lb) combination roughly chopped carrot, celery and onion, some fresh parsley stalks and a bay leaf, and bring to the boil.

✓ When boiling point is reached, reduce heat, and remove scum that has risen to the top of the pot. This is most important - if not removed, your stock will be greasy and cloudy.

✓ Cover with a lid and simmer gently for two hours.

✓ Every twenty minutes or so check that no further grey scum is present, and if it is, remove it.

✓ After two hours, cool stock and strain off. Keep this liquid in small manageable containers in your refrigerator to help you over the next week to make beautiful soups, sauces, gravies and chowders.

salad, warm with bacon and pineapple	30
satay chicken wings	58
sauce bolognese	38
sauce, apple	73
sauce, brown	103
sauce, butter and herb	40
sauce, cheese	103
sauce, mussel and carrageen	44
sauce, spinach and pine nut	40
sauce, tomato	39
scrambled eggs	35
seafood pancakes	52
sesame and honey baklava	92
shortcrust pastry	102
sirloin steak parcels	69
smoked fish and cream cheese paté	44
sole with mussel stuffing	49
soup, carrot and coriander	15
soup, celery and apple	14
soup, iced, roasted tomato	15
soup, nettle	14
spare ribs, barbecued	70
spinach and pine nut sauce	40
sprouts	81
steak and kidney pie	64
steak, pork stuffed	72
steak, sirloin parcels	69
stock, chicken	55
stock, fish	103
stock, meat	12
stock, turkey	104
strawberry mousse	95
stuffed chicken legs	56
stuffed pork steak	72
stuffing, turkey	79
summer pudding	99
sweet sauce with chicken drumsticks	56
tomato sauce	39
tomato roasted, iced	15
trifle, christmas	82
turkey and ham chowder	83
turkey and ham flan	84
turkey breast fried in breadcrumbs	83
turkey breast, roast stuffed	80
turkey gravy	81
turkey legs, roasted and stuffed	80
turkey stock	104
vegetable crumble	23
vegetable lasagne	22
vegetable, hot grilled salad	31
vegetable meal, 1 pot	21
vegetable soup	13
warm salad with bacon and pineapple	30
white/black pudding with apple sauce	73